true belonging

mindful practices to help you
overcome loneliness, connect with
others & cultivate happiness

D0174528

JEFFREY BRANTLEY, MD
WENDY MILLSTINE, NC

New Harbinger Publications, Inc.

Publisher's Note

Distributed in Canada by Raincoast Books

The poem "Tasting Mindfulness" from *Coming to Our Senses: Healing Ourselves and the World through Mindfulness* by Jon Kabat-Zinn, Ph.D, copyright © 2005 Jon Kabat-Zinn, Ph.D. Reprinted by permission of Hyperion. All rights reserved.

The poem "Meditation on the Moment" by Mary Kendall used by permission of the author.

The poem "John" by April Hutchinson used by permission of the author.

Copyright © 2011 by Jeffrey Brantley and Wendy Millstine
          New Harbinger Publications, Inc.
          5674 Shattuck Avenue
          Oakland, CA 94609
          www.newharbinger.com

Cover design by Amy Shoup; Text design by Michele Waters-Kermes; Acquired by Tesilya Hanauer; Edited by Brady Kahn

Library of Congress Cataloging in Publication Data on file

All Rights Reserved. Printed in Canada.

FSC
www.fsc.org
MIX
Paper from
responsible sources
FSC® C011825

13   12   11

10   9   8   7   6   5   4   3   2   1

First printing

This book is printed with soy ink.

This book is dedicated to everyone in our world who feels lost, alone, and hopeless. May you live with peace and ease. May you remember and recover your place in the family of all living things. —J.B.

To my ancestors, whose sacred spirits live within me and connect me to the spiraling cosmos and this marvelous web of life. —W.M.

Contents

introduction

It is often said that we human beings are more alike than we are different.

Not only are we similar in the most basic ways, beginning with our DNA, but we all live our lives in a constantly unfolding present moment—where we are deeply interconnected and interdependent, relying literally breath-by-breath upon physical, emotional, and social exchanges and networks for our very existence and for the fabric of our lives.

Yet, ironically, one of the ways we are most similar is that each of us—given the right conditions—can easily fall victim to a painful, incomplete, and distorting self-view of isolation and disconnection. Such a view is dominated by beliefs and feelings—deeply held—that we are somehow different from those around us or that we are not truly related, or important, to others or that, sadly, we do not belong in this life. In other words, we often get caught in confusion and suffer because of mistaken beliefs about ourselves and about our circumstances.

It could be an extraordinary and beautiful act of good will, self-care, and generosity to learn how to recognize and correct your inaccurate and painful views and feelings of isolation and separation when they arise. It could be a life-changing gift to yourself and to others to learn how to embrace, dwell, rejoice, and act from larger perspectives and experiences of ease and belonging—ones nurtured by your inherent human kindness, intelligence, and compassion.

Who This Book Is For and What It Offers

Have you ever felt isolated or alone? Have you ever suffered, believing that you had become disconnected and were no longer a part of things? Did those feelings of separateness carry with them painful emotions or plunge you into moments of despair or hopelessness?

Most likely, yes! Who has not felt such things? It is part of the suffering that comes with being human.

And, yet, what if you didn't have to be so vulnerable to painful feelings of disconnection or isolation? What if you could learn to remember—and rest more often and more deeply in—the experience of interconnection and the feeling of belonging?

If you have ever felt disconnected or lonely and you long for richer relationships and a deeper sense of connection, this book is for you. A goal of this book is to offer comfort and inspiration. More importantly, this book's goal is to become a resource for liberation and the discovery of new possibilities and joy for anyone trapped in the perception that they are somehow absolutely alone, isolated, or excluded.

Feeling Separated from the Rest

Have you ever wondered what keeps you from connecting more authentically and deeply in each moment—with yourself, with another, or with the flow of your life? Are you ever

3

curious about the obstacles blocking you from more experiences of deep joy and unwavering contentment and belonging? For some insight into these questions, it's necessary to look at the inner world, where feelings like joy and contentment, or disconnection and loneliness, live.

In this inner world of thoughts, feelings, and bodily sensations, you can feel uncomfortably isolated and alone at any time as your life story unfolds. In addition, painful events—such as physical separation, the end of a relationship, the death of a loved one or pet, serious illness, a struggle with addiction, or simply the challenges of living with some deeply personal characteristic like shyness or anxiety—can evoke more thoughts and feelings of disconnection and separation.

Who among us has not been affected by one or more of these challenges in our lives? The experience of loss and vulnerability that we all share is yet another way in which we humans are more alike than we are different.

The demands and challenges of living inevitably call forth thoughts, feelings, and actions every day. These experiences and feelings are also being recorded—as they happen—by the amazing intelligence we have as humans. Later, when something evokes them, or if we remember them on purpose, they can return to the present moment as mind-and-body memories, even if they happened long ago.

As human beings, we are especially prone to recording and remembering experiences associated with danger or threats, real or perceived. For example, you can probably think of a smell, an image, or a sound related to some unpleasant or difficult experience in your past. When you've encountered this cue in your present life, have you ever suddenly felt yourself reliving some or all of that original upsetting experience? Did a suddenly appearing memory disrupt your sense of connection or shift your attention somehow?

If you answered yes, you are not alone. The ability to process threatening or upsetting experiences and then play them back in the present moment as a memory—stimulated by some reminder arising now—is wired into us very deeply as human beings.

When they return, old painful memories in mind and body can seem so real as to ensnare and bind your attention and awareness in habitual patterns of thinking and in strong emotions like grief or anger. Of course, in addition to our life experiences and memories, we humans also tend to add a cognitive inner story, or self-narrative, about what is happening or has happened. The beliefs, opinions, and judgments we carry, whether correct or incorrect, inevitably become key elements and have a strong influence in these evolving story lines.

It can take a lot of courage—plus intentional self-compassion and real skill—to stop, pay attention, and step back from the constant stream of sensations, memories, and stories flowing through you in any given moment. And paying attention more closely means that you must also acknowledge any pain you may be feeling (remembered or otherwise) and perhaps learn to practice self-compassion and self-care more deeply.

It may also require the faith that you really do have a deep reserve of strength as a human being—a place you can turn to inside during challenging times or when facing intense feelings of distress or despair.

Albert Einstein made a remarkable comment in response to a rabbi who had written seeking advice for how to cope with the death of his daughter:

"A human being is part of the whole, called by us 'Universe,' a part limited in time and space. He experiences himself, his thoughts and feelings as something separate from the rest—a kind of optical delusion of his consciousness. This delusion is a kind of prison for us, restricting us to our personal desires and to affection for a few persons nearest to us. Our task must be to free ourselves from this prison by widening our circle of compassion to embrace all living beings and all of nature" (Mitchell 1991, 191–92).

Wait a minute! Is Einstein saying that when any of us experiences loss, aches with grief, or is stuck in personal thoughts and feelings of separation for any reason, we are still (and always) somehow connected and not separate? Connected to whom? Not separate from what? Is he saying that we human beings become easily stuck in how we relate to others and the world because of a limiting and restrictive misunderstanding about being "separate from the rest"?

What if you could investigate Einstein's statement directly through your experience? When having your own thoughts and feelings of being separate from others—no matter what encounter evokes them—what if you could look more deeply and investigate these thoughts and feelings? What if you could see for yourself whether such thoughts and feelings accurately describe how things ultimately and truly are or if they are only an "optical delusion," as Einstein maintains?

You could investigate Einstein's statement. It would take some work and some time and commitment, but you could do it, because you already have what you need. It is another way that we humans are more alike than we are different.

We each have the capacity to be mindful.

Mindfulness

Mindfulness is a core human capacity, and it refers to noticing or knowing what is happening in each moment. For example, when you become aware of a cool breeze striking your face or notice the taste of your favorite ice cream, that moment of awareness of the sensation of the breeze or of knowing you are tasting the ice cream is a mindful moment.

Mindfulness is:

- The awareness of your thoughts; mindfulness does not identify with any thoughts or feelings but is the awareness of them.

- The nonjudging and receptive, allowing and compassionate awareness of present moment experience.

- A capacity you already have; it is always here, at least as a possibility.

༄ A quality that can be cultivated and strength-
ened with practice.

Much as physical exercise can strengthen muscles in the
body, so too can practicing mindfulness cultivate and develop
your natural mindfulness so that this heightened awareness
becomes stronger, more sustainable, and more reliable. Here
practicing does not refer to the usual sense of practicing as a
rehearsal for a competition or performance. Practicing mindfulness means simply intending to show up and pay attention, and doing so repeatedly.

Practicing mindfulness means inviting yourself to engage
and be present for this moment with full and receptive
awareness. It includes bringing to yourself, and to your own
life unfolding in this moment, the same attention, love, and
concern that a mother would bring to watching her child.

Practicing mindfulness means accepting yourself, too, as
not being perfect or always mindful or caring, even as you
do your best—as often as you can—to embody an orienta-
tion of attention with calmness, nonjudging acceptance, and
equanimity, right here and now. For example, as a mindful
practice, you could choose repeatedly to pay attention for a
time to the direct sensations of your breathing, learning to
work patiently with your mind when it wanders and continuing to observe gently the changing sensations as your body
inhales and exhales.

Alternatively, you could practice mindfulness by pausing
and noticing—totally accepting and allowing—the particular
quality of your mind in this moment. Noticing, for example,

is it alert? Interested? Chatting? Sleepy? Not identifying with the condition or fighting it or trying to change it in any way. Simply letting it be as it is, as you notice and allow it.

Practicing mindfulness allows you to uncouple from mistaken beliefs and views that may be fixed in your heart and mind. It can help you do this because, as you become more mindful, you can become more conscious of your state of mind and its contents without becoming lost in thoughts or feelings.

The reading and practices in this book will help you to increase your mindfulness of your thoughts, feelings, and bodily sensations. As you read and explore the practices, you will realize how mindfulness can have an enormous positive impact upon your capacity to see clearly, connect more fully, and respond more deeply and compassionately in any situation or moment, whether that situation or moment be a challenging or an enjoyable one.

How Mindfulness Can Nurture Connections and Relationships

When facing a challenge, a threatening person, or a difficult situation, in what direction and how do your mind and heart move? Do they move toward the experience, alert and open, or away from it, closed and hard?

Challenging experiences have the power to evoke a wide spectrum of feelings and thoughts in your inner world. Freedom—to connect and relate with authenticity—lies not in constantly seeking ways to avoid or escape such challenging experiences (which is basically not possible, anyway), but in increasing your capacity to dwell more unshakably and alertly in the present and to recognize and manage more consciously your reactions to your experience as it unfolds.

How many times in a conversation or social situation have you heard or asked, "Who do you think you are?" This question usually explodes into the present moment when someone has said or done something that suddenly offends or threatens the very fabric of a relationship. Where did the offending words or actions come from?

What was happening in this person's inner life just before he gave offense and it became obvious to everyone else? And frankly, who has not asked herself, *What was I thinking?* or *Who did I think I was when I said [or did] that?* What was happening in your inner life just before you said or did what you then questioned?

By learning to dwell more unshakably, alertly, and mindfully in the present moment, you can grow in self-awareness and better manage unconscious and impulsive words and deeds. You can identify more choices, recognize more connections, and gain confidence and ease for deepening your relationships with others and taking your rightful place in the world.

Practicing mindfulness allows you to recognize that you really do have a choice in how you react to the changing conditions within, in relationships with others, and in the world around you. It offers the refuge, strength, and possibility that follow from clear seeing with compassionate awareness, disentangled from distorted perceptions or mistaken beliefs, moment by moment.

Practicing mindfulness can also help nurture relationships and connections, for it helps you recognize when an exaggerated self-centered view has solidified inside and your ego's demands and story line have become too loud. Practicing mindfulness in those moments can help you experience yourself as larger than you may have believed yourself to be, and perhaps wiser, too. It can help you respond from a perspective beyond your unique personality's story and ego needs, without disrespecting or devaluing your own particularity in any way.

Mindfulness can help you recognize and let go of the self-centered perspective when it becomes too demanding, constricting, or distorting. It can help you relate from a much larger space of awareness that is inherently deeply present and in touch with each moment.

True Belonging

Do you long to feel, throughout your body and your entire being, a deep sense of peace and ease—one that holds you and is a refuge that allows connection and a sense of belonging, in any situation and any moment, no matter how challenging? Perhaps you could feel this way. Perhaps you already have felt this way.

This feeling of peace and ease might be at once beautifully mysterious and inexpressible in words. It could appear as an act of grace or as a manifestation of benevolence, suddenly, in this moment.

Maybe, at some deep level, you also realize that you cannot summon it or make such a profound experience automatically appear. Yet you might also know very deeply and confidently that there are nutrients, some elements or skills, which would invite this experience more often into your life if you added them.

For example, such a feeling of ease and belonging could depend on the skills of intention, attention, and acceptance. These skills, as you practice them, empower you to remain present within each moment, linking you to your basic intelligence and goodness as a human being and enabling you to steadily notice what is happening, without becoming reactive or entangled in it.

When that beautiful and mysterious feeling appears and saturates your entire being, then you might call such a feeling of complete ease and presence—of recognition, appreciation, and the experience of a felt reality of connection and relationship, regardless of circumstances—true belonging. And true belonging could be experienced in many, many ways.

It could be the ease and confidence arising deep in your heart during the direct experience of pausing, opening, allowing, and feeling in touch with what is happening in your inner world and the outer one, breath by breath.

It could be the felt experience of an unwavering dimension of inner peace and safety in each moment of your life, regardless of conditions or circumstances.

Or it could mean becoming so acutely conscious and relaxed about your participation in and contribution to the unfolding tapestry of the present moment, of knowing with such certainty that you are already so deeply and inextricably bound up in that vibrant, enormous fabric, that you stop believing any doubts in your own mind or heart to the contrary.

Or, simply, true belonging could be the undeniable realization—in an instant, at the deepest levels of your being—of your profound similarity and commonality with even one single other living thing: a wondrous, insightful "they are like me / I am like them" moment.

Our deep hope and intention in writing this book is that as you read the narratives here and, most importantly, you try and directly experience at least some of the practices, you will gain increased understanding, a deeper sense of connection, and greater peace and happiness. And we hope and intend that you will be guided and inspired by that experience in some mysterious way so that, just possibly, our world and others in it may benefit more than ever from the beauty of your life.

Habitual, Limiting Views

Following the path to realizing true belonging and greater happiness could begin—in any moment—with a simple shift in perspective, of expanding your frame of reference beyond your familiar sense of self and the habitual and conditioned demands of your personality.

To begin, it is helpful to recall that your personality is heavily weighted toward self-interest and self-oriented views—as are the personalities of all of us, in fact! Your personality is thus easily mobilized into full and loud expression of its demands and opinions. Furthermore, those demands are often based on mistaken beliefs about who you are—or, perhaps, who your personality thinks it is.

But this is not to say that there's anything wrong with having a personality or wrong with anyone's unique personality! Quite the opposite, in fact. Much of the richness and joy of life are reflected each moment in the beautiful diversity that arises as unique personalities interact and express themselves in the world. Furthermore, expanding your capacity for opening to and connecting with widely different expressions of life, including different types of people, can actually be a powerful means of experiencing deeper connections and true belonging.

However, when a self-centered view arises—a view that is driven by mistaken ideas or by greed, neediness, fear, or other less attractive elements in the personality—and begins to dictate your thoughts, words, and actions, then there can be real problems, real suffering, for you and for anyone in relationship with you. These difficult elements arise in everyone, of course, and they have the power to dictate your perspective, perceptions, and intentions, breath by breath.

If you really think about it, noticing and listening to those inner comments, at some point you might wonder: *Which person in my personality is actually speaking?* You have probably heard generous, kind, and wise voices speaking as your personality, as well as greedy, needy, fearful, and hateful ones!

At any moment, any of those voices could be adding to an old and well-established self-view or perception, which is busily and authoritatively telling you in a particular, familiar, and limiting way who (it thinks) you are or explaining (from its perspective) what is happening. To illustrate the enormous power of habitual and limiting self-views—and the self-narratives or stories that support them and shape ongoing experience—here are two common examples: self-views related to loneliness and self-views connected with sad or depressed moods.

Loneliness is a word often associated with the painful feeling of separation. A large body of research affirms that "feeling lonely" is bad for your health and has been associated with a variety of mental and physical disorders and even premature death (Hafen, Karren, Frandsen, and Smith 1996, 298). However, research also affirms that the feeling of loneliness is due more to a person's interior experience, including habits of thinking and feeling and self-perception, than to outer circumstances. In other words, feelings of loneliness are strongly connected to and depend to a large extent upon a particular limited view that some people have of themselves.

Many lonely people have distinctive personal characteristics, such as an inability to be assertive, extreme shyness, or exceeding self-consciousness, that make it difficult for them to form and maintain relationships (Hafen and Frandsen 1987). Additionally, such factors as low self-esteem, a perception of being surrounded by people who don't seem lonely, or a sense of not belonging to an accepting community are all associated with worse feelings of loneliness (Blai 1989). Each of these factors arises from a pattern of interior judgments, personal perceptions, and behaviors that are activated moment by moment.

Epidemiologist Leonard A. Sagan has pointed out that the number of people you surround yourself with is not as important as the satisfaction you get from your relationships and whether or not you perceive that you are isolated (Sagan 1987). Your perceptions of the world around you are clearly and directly related to your inner story or commentary about your experiences and your interactions with others.

Another example of the power of unconsciously held perspectives, or how mistaken beliefs about yourself can shape your experience, comes from studies of people with depression. Depressed people are more likely to misinterpret an ambiguous social situation as a negative comment on their own worth. This is due to the fact that sad moods can reactivate vulnerable thoughts, beliefs, and negative attitudes, which influence the self-view people hold and how they experience their interactions with others (Segal, Williams, and Teasdale, 2002).

To illustrate, imagine this scene: A person, seeing someone across the street whom she thinks she knows, waves. The other person keeps on walking without responding. In this ambiguous situation, if the person waving is in a depressed (or sad) mood, she is likely to interpret the failure to wave back as meaning that the person across the street is avoiding her on purpose. She might very well then descend and become stuck, perhaps for quite a while, in an intense and critical internal self-story that asserts conclusively that she is unattractive and no one likes her.

If she were not in a depressed mood, this person might decide instead that the other person was not who she thought she was or that this person didn't see her. She would shrug her shoulders and move on. How any of us responds to such a situation (and similar ones happen all the time) depends "on the story we tell ourselves, the running commentary in the mind that interprets the data we receive through our senses" (Williams, Teasdale, Segal, and Kabat-Zinn 2007, 20).

Of course, personalities are complex, and there is more to loneliness and depression than the story you tell yourself.

However, the research is clear that the meaning people give to their experience is closely related to how they unconsciously or consciously talk to themselves about what is happening within and without, based on a set of interior narratives or story lines. The inner view you are upholding, based in beliefs and opinions as well as memories and other elements of your personal history, has an enormous impact on your perceptions of your unfolding experience and relationship with life, including whether you see or feel connections and a sense of belonging or you instead feel increasingly isolated and distressed.

These findings from psychology appear to be a variation on the theme of Einstein's optical delusion, and they point back to a common vulnerability—and a deep similarity—we humans share. Although we are interdependent and interconnected beings living in complex ecological and social networks and relationships, we can simultaneously become prisoners of a deep misunderstanding and misperception of separation and isolation. We are forgetful of these interconnections when our attention is drawn into intense interior feelings or compelling and disturbing self-centered, selfish thoughts.

Each moment, therefore, offers an opportunity. With the help of mindfulness, you can learn to recognize these habitual and limiting views and inner narratives, meet them with kindness and compassion, disentangle from their grip, and move to a larger perspective that immediately illuminates and sustains you.

Expanding Your Perspectives

How might you expand your perspectives beyond the habitual, reactive perceptions that narrow and limit your relationships and experience of yourself and others and of life itself?

What if—whenever you became entangled in harsh inner tension and the mistaken perception that you are not connected, nor loved or loveable, or that you have been left behind, abandoned, and are all alone—you could disentangle from those perceptions, beliefs, and reactions and open into a larger perspective that is immediately more gentle, generous, and life affirming?

What if you learned to pause and shift your view and started paying attention to what was happening in your mind and body not as "you" at all but simply as changing experience?

What if you could find some way to observe your interior environment—including any upset you felt—more spaciously and generously, with greater awareness and without becoming stuck in the usual mental and emotional reactions? What if you could relax more and stop taking the changing conditions of your inner life so personally? What if you could embrace yourself more reliably and more often with love, respect, and compassion?

Wouldn't that be an expanded perspective?

Building a New Perspective

Perspective—the view, or frame of reference, you are holding in a given moment—is crucial to your experience. Perspective can act as a filter, limiting or even distorting what is noticed and how you make sense of or respond to the changing conditions in a given situation.

It is widely known that what any of us thinks we know is rarely a complete, or completely accurate, representation of whatever is the subject of our attention.

Learning to release the personality's grip (what we think we know) on any narrow perspective, on any subject—setting down and relaxing the view dictated by the rigidly held opinions of the ego-mind—immediately opens each of us to a much vaster and more mysterious universe of possibilities and meanings, alive in each moment.

In this book, and especially in the practices, we are inviting you to adopt and explore an expanded, perhaps somewhat radical, view—beyond the usual, familiar, and habitual thoughts and feelings—of who you are, who you can be, and how you might live and relate to yourself and to others. In other words, we are inviting you to consider the possibility that you might actually be larger and more beautiful and generous as a human being than you, perhaps, have ever dreamed you were!

We encourage you to enter and live intentionally from this expanded frame of reference and to see for yourself if this larger view resonates with you, helps you find more peace and joy in living, and promotes more richness and a deeper, felt sense of belonging in all of your relationships.

It's Up to You

A liberating shift in perspective is possible, and it could actually be yours. To make this shift, you need to be willing to learn and to do a certain kind of inner work: paying close attention to your senses, perceptions, and thoughts; being totally present when facing challenges in your life; and keeping your attention steady and your heart open, no matter what is happening.

The sense of connection and belonging we point to is not an abstraction. It is to be experienced directly and is only truly understood through your direct experience.

Ultimately, it's up to you to find out for yourself how true belonging feels and what it means as a support and source of strength in your life.

How To Use This Book

You might begin by approaching this book and its practices as you would a friend who has your best interests at heart, a friend who is there for you with a warm hand, clear mind, and open heart. There are many possibilities waiting for you here. They can unfold, be revealed, and support you in myriad and perhaps unsuspected ways if you let yourself move deeply and steadily into them through the readings, reflections, and practices.

The Foundation chapter that follows will provide you with a strong base of information to guide and support you as you prepare to engage in and explore the mindfulness-based practices for connection and belonging. The practices are organized into three parts: Connecting with Yourself, Connecting with Others, and Taking Mindful and Compassionate Action in the World. You will find that the practices support each other.

You may work through the parts of this book in any order you choose. You can move around, pick a practice you like, or begin with the one that calls most immediately and powerfully to you. You could even pick a different practice each day and start like that.

And you can relax as you practice. You won't make a mistake or break anything!

As you do the practices, it will help if you let go of judgments and expectations. There is no right or wrong way to do them, and your experience may surprise you, so you can just let go and open into your practices, enjoying them, exploring, and allowing things to be revealed.

In other words, just do the practices that call to you and see what happens. Do them repeatedly if you are inclined.

We encourage you to approach this book, and especially the practices you engage in, as an unfolding journey of discovery and understanding, and to allow the revelations and teachings you find to amaze, strengthen, inform, illuminate, and expand you.

So then, what does true belonging really mean for you? What will it come to mean? How will it inform and inspire you? Perhaps the time has come to find out.

Welcome, read on, and warm good wishes.

the foundation

Here is an example of an expanded perspective you might consider.

> Life happens only in the present moment, and the wonder and mystery of life is available only here and now.
>
> The unfolding expression of life in the present moment is one of constantly fluxing and changing patterns of complex interrelatedness. That expression includes each of us, with our deeply conditioned personal psycho-biological continuum of thoughts, feelings, and bodily sensations, as well as our awareness and intentions, and our depths of human heart and spirit, moment by moment.
>
> Bringing the present moment and our changing interior experiences more consciously into awareness—breath by breath—provides new opportunities for more skillful, wiser, and more compassionate action. Increased awareness invites a deeper embrace of responsibility for personal actions, and illuminates a greater capacity to help others. All this arises from the direct recognition of the deeply interconnected nature of human, and indeed, all life.

And here is an exercise to illustrate the lightning speed with which perspective can contract around the self-centered view, which is not a permanent identity and not always present but can, nonetheless, arise and impose its particular beliefs and direct our intentions, thoughts, and actions in any moment.

1. Assume you are in a canoe on a fog-covered lake, paddling quietly, gliding over the water. Suddenly, you hear a loud thump behind you and feel a jolt, rocking your canoe.

2. What happens in your mind? Perhaps a string of angry words or a sense of being assaulted arises? *Who ran into me? Who hit me?* Angrily, you turn to face the intruder.

3. When you look, there is a boat floating behind you. You notice it is empty and that the mooring rope appears to be dangling in the water. Instantly, you recognize that you have been struck by an empty boat adrift on the lake.

4. What happens now in your mind? Does the anger of the last moment suddenly disappear? Does the sense of insult vanish when you realize that you are not under attack by anyone and that nothing personal has happened?

What if you could get some relief from that quickly arising, reactive sense of insult and threat? What if you could recognize the appearance and presence of the familiar I-me-mine self-centered view with more humor, and some tolerance, and take it less seriously, not criticizing or blaming yourself in any way for having a self-view that is so strong?

In order to explore these questions further, you will need to look more deeply and closely at how views, actions, and the connections among all of us interrelate and how you can deliberately cultivate the power of mindfulness in your life, so you can access and act from your deepest and best places as a human being.

How You See It Matters: Perspectives on Self, Change, and Connection

The present moment of your life, when you really stop and notice it, is filled with constantly changing conditions.

Of course, there are the changing conditions and situations around you: sights, sounds, smells, people, and so on. None of these lasts. You cannot hold on to them.

But when you really pay attention and look a little deeper, don't you also notice that the closer, more intimate experiences—those in your inner life of mind and body—are also constantly changing? For example, you can notice how the in-and-out sensations of your breath are changing; how the position of your body is changing, whether standing or sitting, reclining or walking; and, when you stop and observe them, how your moods and emotions and your very thoughts are also constantly changing.

And isn't it also true that these intimate, vacillating inner experiences of mind and body are often not seen clearly, if at all?

It is all too easy to mistake a strong feeling (like anger, worry, fear, sadness, or grief) or a familiar thought pattern (like self-criticism or a painful memory) happening now, in this moment, as something solid or constant, or as an identity, as "me." For example, when feeling anxious or sad, you might say, "I am an anxious person" or "I am a depressed person," as if that were who you are and the condition were some unchanging singularity that defines you.

More likely, you have not noticed the many other times when you were not anxious or sad, or you have become so distracted by anxiety or sadness that you fail to notice the other elements of your life experience that are also present here and now, in this moment.

And, when you really look closely at them, even intense feelings and mental stories, like those associated with anger, worry, anxiety, or sadness and grief, are continuously changing.

Refuge and Relief in the Face of Constant Change

Where could you (or anyone) find deeper peace and understanding, constancy, refuge, or true belonging in the flux of outer and inner conditions, in this reality of impermanence and constant change? How could any of us happily live our lives knowing we cannot hold on to anyone or anything?

Perhaps the secret lies in learning how to become more at home, at ease, accepting, and wise about the truth of constant change. Consider the perspective of Jon Kabat-Zinn in his poem (2005, 242):

Tasting Mindfulness

Have you ever had the experience of stopping so
    completely,
of being in your body so completely,
of being in your life so completely,
that what you knew and what you didn't know,
that what had been and what was yet to come,
and the way things are right now
no longer held even the slightest hint of anxiety or
    discord?
It would be a moment of complete presence, beyond
    striving, beyond mere acceptance,
beyond the desire to escape or fix anything or plunge
    ahead,
a moment of pure being, no longer in time,
a moment of pure seeing, pure feeling,
a moment in which life simply is,
and that "isness" grabs you by all your senses,
all your memories, by your very genes,
by your loves, and
welcomes you home.

In other words, in the midst of constant change, could it be that what must stop is you? Is it possible that the only thing that could stop is you? Or perhaps, some part of you, a part that can be known, is already stopped and is merely waiting to be found?

Could stopping be about something more than stopping your hurrying and busyness in body and mind? Could it also be about keeping your heart open and developing an attention that can be still and remain focused as it gives access to a vast awareness that allows you to be conscious of, but not limited to, your changing thoughts and emotions?

What if, with that awareness, you were able to notice, include, and allow all these changes without having to change or become disturbed?

Kabat-Zinn is pointing us (as have countless teachers before him) to the possibility that deep peace is available and is related to learning to stop in a remarkably human way, one that enables you to be aware and conscious in your mind and body, in your life, and in each moment with "complete presence."

What if when you noticed your mind telling you a story about how lonely or isolated you are—and when you noticed upset feelings in your mind or body in that moment—you could hold those stories and feelings in awareness and maintain the view that they are not the whole truth of who you are or what is happening?

What if, even as you are feeling upset or pain in mind or body—noticing and holding it very kindly and mindfully in awareness—you could also mindfully notice and appreciate the amazing array of interconnections continuously maintaining your life and linking you with so many others? What if you could also see all of you together in the now, living and participating, moment by moment, in an unfolding, dynamic reality that includes multiple living systems and relationships, including ones within your own mind and body?

Remembering to Notice, Paying Attention, and Flexing Your View

Becoming more skeptical of subjective perceptions of being disconnected or alone—learning to look more closely at threads of interconnection and interdependency operating in each moment—could become a strategy that supports you in times of stress or danger. Increasing your flexibility at shifting your perceptions could also help you restore balance to your life or become more skilled at deepening the relationships that are yours to enjoy.

Opening to, noticing, and directly perceiving the threads of interdependency operating in your life, moment by moment, depends in large measure on your being willing and able to stop, relax, and look more deeply (notice) as things are happening (revealing themselves) here and now.

Here is a simple example to illustrate the many points about view, perceptions, and interconnectedness being explored here:

Imagine that you are about to eat an apple. As you look closely at the apple in your hand, what do you see? How did that apple come to be in your hand? What are the elements present now, what brought them here, and what is unfolding in this moment?

For example, the apple represents the growth of a seed into a fruit-bearing tree that was nourished by light, moisture, nutrients, and many other things. The tree bore fruit that was picked and prepared by someone and transported somehow to a market or fruit stand, where you likely purchased it with money you had earned from doing something for someone else in another series of relationships. Once the apple is in your hand, the different systems of your own mind and body become involved to bite, chew, swallow, and digest the apple and absorb its nutrients.

And that is only part of the story. You can reflect on other dimensions in this apple-biting present moment. For example, where did the apple seed come from? How did you learn to do what you did to earn the money to buy the apple? How did you get to the place where you bought the apple?

On one level, all this can seem like an abstraction, but on another level, if you look deeply enough, can you envision the seed, the sunlight, the workers' touch, and all of the other elements in the long body of events behind the apple you are now holding? Without any of these elements, the apple would be different or would not be there at all.

Now imagine biting the apple. What is happening now? What do you taste? What do you smell? What is happening in your mouth and in other parts of your body? As you move through this imaginary exercise of mindfully eating an apple, you may well ask, *Where does the apple stop and where do I begin?* Especially once you have eaten the apple!

With close and steady attention, the individual elements and conditions, seemingly separate in a given moment, can actually be observed to be interrelated and interconnected, changing and contributing to the next moment, in its different appearances and forms, and those to the next, and so on. Therefore, are you and the apple actually separate after all?

Learning to stop, rest, and flex your view in this particular way—noticing the interconnectedness in experience that is changing every moment—also could mean learning how not to put any experience, or anyone, out of your heart, and how to recognize and not be unconsciously driven by feelings of ill will and aversion toward upsetting or challenging experiences as they appear in the unfolding present.

Stopping and relaxing into Kabat-Zinn's "moment of pure being" might require learning to keep your heart receptive and open and to cultivate self-compassion as well as compassion for others. And it could include acquiring access to a powerful inner source of strength, courage, and equanimity that allows you to remain, breath by breath, present, inclusive, and conscious of any experience or condition you are facing, no matter how challenging.

Nourishing and strengthening mindfulness can help you develop the ability to be truly present in your life and for your life as it unfolds. You can practice mindfulness more often, and in practicing, you can actually change your views and perspectives, as well as how your brain and nervous system operate and how your body responds in a variety of situations.

Cultivating Mindfulness

You can cultivate mindfulness and practice your art of presence through formal meditation methods, such as those provided in this book or other methods that you may already know about. You also can learn to extend mindfulness informally by practicing during everyday moments and situations. Practicing informally in the reality of daily living can lead to illuminating insights and shifts in perspective that empower you to engage your total life experience with more awareness, understanding, and the possibility for more effective action.

Because the practices that appear later in this book depend upon mindfulness as a crucial and unifying element, this portion of the Foundation is devoted to teaching you more about mindfulness, including a brief set of instructions for a core mindfulness-of-breathing practice. You may wish to refer back to these instructions from time to time for support as you engage in mindful breathing in the different practices that follow.

This poem by Mary Kendall offers a glimpse of the experience of mindful breathing:

Meditation on the Moment

When I am ready,
I close my eyes
and focus on the breathing;
awareness of air
passing through the nose
down through the body;

the belly rises, falls,
rises again—
its slow rhythm
setting the tone.

Next, focus on the body,
accepting it for once
as it is right now,
here in this moment,
for the moment
is all we have.

Breathing in,
breathing out,
shoulders soft,
no striving
to get somewhere,
for there is no place
to be but here.

No judging of self,
simply letting it be
in the moment
for the moment.

Rain pounds against the glass
this February evening.
The image begins with sound
transforming into a thought.

Raindrops falling,
each one perfectly formed
but then releasing,
allowing itself to lose
what it was alone,
becoming instead
part of something more.

One Mindfulness, Many Methods

You can be mindful of just about anything! Awareness of your breathing is only one example. Mindfulness arises when you pay attention on purpose to any experience with an attitude of acceptance, allowing what you are noticing to be as it is without trying to fix it or change it in any way.

It is also helpful to have a method of practicing mindfulness that you can call upon whenever you realize that you are not being mindful or when you simply wish to practice mindfulness more formally for its own sake. The mindfulness-of-breathing practice is one such method.

Any method you use for practicing mindfulness will involve choosing a focus, which could be narrow or very wide, for your attention and then knowing how to work with your mind when it wanders off of the focus or becomes lost in thought. For example, when practicing mindfulness of breathing, attention is placed on the sensations of your body breathing, doing this with an attitude of accepting what is happening and letting things be as they are. Acceptance of experience, breath by breath, includes noticing when your mind wanders into thinking and then—with patience and kindness—intentionally returning your attention to focus on the breath sensations.

Mindfulness of breathing will remain a foundation practice as you move on to explore different objects of attention for practicing mindfulness. Other practices in the book will invite you to explore placing the focus of mindful attention in a variety of ways and in different situations to promote your sense of discovery and appreciation for the connections in your life and the interrelatedness of all things.

Mindfulness Is for Everybody

These days, you are likely to hear about mindfulness in many places. Although it has often been mistakenly identified as exclusively a Buddhist concept, mindfulness is a basic human capacity, relied upon in a variety of faith traditions. More recently, it has also been the subject of interventions and research in health and scientific communities.

In faith traditions besides Buddhism, the qualities of awareness, stillness, and nonjudging attention are valued and can be found. For example, the practice of *centering prayer* in Christianity intends to develop an inner stillness to promote deeper communion with God. On the Jewish holy day of Shabbat, there is a core intention of rest from busyness and of abstention from labor. Many sources in Hinduism value stillness of mind and steady attention. An example is from the Katha Upanishad: "When all the senses are stilled, when the mind is at rest, when the intellect wavers not, then, say the wise, is reached the highest state." The Chinese Taoist master Lao-Tzu advised, "Empty your mind of all thoughts. Let your heart be at peace."

During the past thirty years or so in the West, the qualities of being centered in the present moment, nonjudging attention, and expanded awareness—all associated with mindfulness—have also gained broad interest among a variety of health providers and researchers, sparked in large part by pioneers like Jon Kabat-Zinn, who developed mindfulness-based stress reduction (MBSR) (1990), and Marsha Linehan, who created dialectical behavior therapy (DBT) (1993).

Specifically, MBSR teaches individuals to become active partners in their own health and healing by bringing mindfulness practice to a wide variety of stress-related and medical or psychological conditions, and DBT offers extensive training to help those with problems of emotion regulation and impulsive behavior cope more effectively and live happier lives.

Numerous scientific studies have now identified benefits of mindfulness and meditation in coping with a range of conditions, from stress and chronic pain to anxiety and relapse prevention in both chronic depression and addictions therapy (Kabat-Zinn 2005; Shapiro and Carlson 2009; Didonna 2009).

As you can see, the world of mindfulness is vast and rich. We hope you will be inspired by your experience with the readings, references, and practices in this book to delve more and more deeply into it.

Developing the Skills of Mindfulness

Although you have mindfulness naturally, strengthening the three mindfulness skills of intention, attention, and nonjudging attitude can assist you in realizing the vast possibilities that mindfulness offers.

Intention simply means knowing about mindfulness and intending to be mindful by practicing with formal meditation and, informally, in the many different situations and moments of daily living.

Attention is all about focus. A core aspect of all meditation practices is concentration, and concentration means you focus the mind—focus your attention—on an object of experience. You might choose a narrow focus for attention, such as following closely the minute sensations associated with each breath and disregarding all other experiences. Or you might choose a broader focus—one that is more inclusive—for example, being open and noticing all the different sounds you are hearing; or holding the breath sensations more lightly so that they become a kind of anchor for attention as you also include thoughts, bodily sensations, and sounds in your noticing of moment-by-moment experience.

An important lesson to learn in meditation is that attention is trainable, through practice, to be steadier and stronger so that it can be sustained upon any object or focus you choose. Whenever you are practicing mindfulness, and notice your mind has wandered, each time you bring your attention back to your focus (to a breath sensation, for example), you are actually training your attention to be steadier and stronger.

Having a *nonjudging attitude* means that, as you pay attention, you assume a stance or outlook of allowing whatever is happening and of being friendly and receptive to what is noticed. You can practice these qualities, too. For example, you can develop a nonjudging attitude by becoming mindful when your mind is judging, neither feeding that habit nor judging yourself for being judgmental. Or you can deliberately cultivate an attitude of kindness and openheartedness in many ways through your meditations and actions. (Later in this book, you will find practices for cultivating kindness and related qualities of the heart.)

Making Compatible Lifestyle Choices

If you wish to bring mindfulness forward in your life, it is important to understand how the lifestyle choices and other behaviors you make might impact your practice, either in positive ways or in ways that interfere with mindfulness. For example, if your intention in practicing mindfulness is to make yourself feel a certain way (such as calm) or not feel a certain way (such as sad), then you might tend to practice mindfulness only when such feelings are already present. This is not only a mistaken understanding of mindfulness (for one thing, your practice is being driven by judging and striving), but it means that you are most likely not even thinking about or developing your intention about being mindful (or your mindfulness practice) in the moments when such feelings are not present.

Certain lifestyle choices can hamper your ability to develop the skill of attention. If you take intoxicants to excess, habitually overeat before meditating, or are chronically sleep deprived, then when you sit to meditate, your nervous system and entire body are having to manage a heavy input of distraction that is unnecessary and can interfere with your practice by making you feel dull, drowsy, or otherwise numb to this moment.

Finally, cultivating a nonjudging and receptive attitude may be more challenging if you tend to dwell on feelings of anger and resentment. If you fill your thoughts with those energies and express them through judgmental and critical words and actions, then how can you expect such habits of thinking and feeling to simply disappear just because you decide to sit and meditate for half an hour?

A more skillful approach might be to let mindfulness support you and allow yourself to notice and consciously acknowledge whenever your mind is filling with anger and resentment. Then, more conscious of the anger, you might begin to consider or choose a different response; or you might decide to investigate what lies beneath the anger or ill will that you feel. Such investigation could perhaps lead to deeper self-awareness and guide you in a next step—for instance, to the need to practice forgiveness for yourself and for others.

As your mindfulness practice unfolds over time, you will likely notice how some of your choices and actions help to grow and support your practice and how others may work against it. You may also find that changing old habits and making new choices will become more natural and easy at some point, informed by the awareness of your process.

Working with Thoughts (and Other Wanderings of Your Mind)

Your mind will wander when you are practicing mindfulness. When that happens, remember that you have not made a mistake or done anything wrong. It happens to everyone. You do not have to control your thoughts or blank your mind, and you do not have to follow or feed the thoughts. Just relax and bring your attention back to your focus.

Much of the practice of mindfulness involves the training of attention and the understanding of how your mind works. Such understanding actually follows from noticing the wandering mind repeatedly, not getting lost either in fighting it or in following it, and reestablishing your focus and your practice, breath by breath.

A useful tool when practicing mindfulness, especially if your mind is busy, having difficulty with concentration, or easily distracted, is to employ the technique of silently naming what you notice. Here is how this works. As you are being mindful, when you notice something, you silently (as if whispering to yourself) note what is happening, using very simple names.

For example, while maintaining most of your attention on feeling the direct sensation of your breath, you might begin to whisper lightly and silently to yourself "in" on the in-breath; "stillness" or "pause" when you notice the ending of the in-breath; "out" at the beginning of the out-breath sensation; and "stillness" or "pause" at the end of the out-breath; letting yourself feel the actual experience of each breath sensation arising from stillness and returning there as you silently name what you are feeling, just as the feeling arises.

You can add this soft and gentle noting to other experiences, as well, as they arise in your awareness. For example, you might whisper "hearing" when your attention moves to sounds, or "thinking" (or name "worrying," "planning," "remembering," and so on when different types of thoughts appear). You may also quietly name different sensations in your body, using terms like "pressure," "vibration," "heat," "contraction," or "dryness."

You can relax as you practice noticing and naming. Allow your attention to become more and more sensitive. Let the naming happen precisely as the sensation arises or as soon as you notice it. When another experience arises, name that, releasing the previous one.

As you name what is happening, remember to let the silent naming be only about 5 percent of your attention and mental activity. You should maintain the bulk of your quiet attention on the direct experience of what you are noticing.

This naming is a skillful use of thoughts to help focus and stabilize attention while practicing mindfulness. At some point, you might find that even this 5 percent thinking is no longer necessary and is distracting. At that point, you can simply drop the naming and rest completely in the quiet watching-and-knowing of what is happening. Remember that you don't *have* to note and name with mental labels. Use the naming practice only if it is helpful.

How to Use Mindfulness of Breathing

Often in the practices in the next section, you will find a reference to "mindfulness of breathing" or directions to "breathe mindfully" as part of the practice. Here are some basic instructions for practicing mindfulness of breathing. You can use them in the practices, or you could build a meditation practice on them, doing both formal periods of meditation and, more informally, breathing mindfully in the changing circumstances of daily living.

Of course, if you are already familiar with mindfulness of breathing or have an established practice already, feel free to use your own method of practice.

You can practice mindfulness of breathing in any posture—sitting, standing, moving, or lying down. Try them all out! You will also want to practice mindfulness of breathing as your body is moving at different speeds, noticing the interrelationships of the moving body and the moving mind.

∽ core practice:
Mindfulness of Breathing

To practice mindfulness of breathing, simply do the following:

1. Consciously intend and decide to practice mindfulness of breathing.

2. If you are doing formal practice, choose a place where you are unlikely to be disturbed, and take a position that supports your body comfortably and encourages alertness.

3. Remembering that mindfulness is about being and not doing, about noticing how things are, and about coming back to direct experience, allow yourself to put down the busyness, the doing, and the becoming of everyday life. For the time of this meditation, drop into this moment, letting yourself rest in awareness, simply being present to your experience.

4. Bring your attention to the sensations in your body, arising and flowing through your awareness in this moment. Notice pressure, heaviness, expansion, vibration, heat, cold, and so on. No need to do anything. Let yourself relax and simply notice

the changing sensations, allowing them to come to you, change, and leave, each sensation replaced by another.

5. When you have gathered attention in your body, are settled in, and are feeling steadier in the noticing of the changing flow of sensations, gently bring your attention to the sensations of breathing.

6. Let your attention rest at the place in your body where you feel each breath sensation most easily. You don't have to search or force anything. You can relax. There is no way to make a mistake. The sensations of this breath may be felt most easily at your nose or your mouth, or they may be felt in your chest or your abdomen or someplace else. There is no right or wrong. See where the sensations are most clearly felt for you and rest your attention there.

7. Let your attention become increasingly precise and sensitive so that you may begin to notice different aspects of the changing sensations, such as the beginning, the middle, and the end of the in-breath, a pause, and the beginning, the middle, and the end of the out-breath, and another pause.

8. Notice long breaths and short ones. Notice deep breaths and shallow ones. Be interested and curious about what each breath is like. You don't have to worry about the last breath or the next one. Just relax and let your attention rest on this breath, this experience, this moment.

9. You don't have to do anything special. You can relax. Let the breath come to you. You do not have to control your breath in any way. This is an awareness practice, not a breathing exercise. Trust your body to breathe, however it needs to, while you maintain attention and awareness of the changing flow of sensations in each breath.

10. When your mind wanders, remember: you don't have to fight or control your thoughts, and you do not have to follow or feed them, either. You have not made a mistake when your mind wanders; it is what your mind does! Practicing the attitudes of kindness, nonjudging awareness, and patience, gently and repeatedly bring your attention back to the experience of this breath each time you notice the mind wandering.

11. If it helps, you could practice the technique of silently naming your experience. Work with this technique for a while, noticing if

your attention steadies or becomes more precise as a result. Practice naming as long as you like, always without forcing it and without trying to change anything that is happening. The naming simply helps focus attention. When you wish, drop the naming and simply rest, quietly and completely, in the watching-and-knowing awareness.

12. Practice for as long as you like, using the technique of silently naming or not, as you choose, and returning attention to the sensations of this breath whenever you need to. To end your meditation, simply return your attention to your surroundings.

You will probably have to bring your attention back to the breath many, many times as you meditate. The meditation is not so much about being with the breath every single second as it is about how you notice and come back.

It helps to remember that the wandering of your mind is only a habit pattern, and when you notice it and bring attention back from where it wanders, you diminish the power of that habit and increase your capacity to sustain attention in the present moment and to connect directly with the experience of being alive in this moment.

Over time, the mindfulness-of-breathing meditation practice helps you develop space around your thoughts, your feelings, and your sensations and to discern them accurately and compassionately. Such discernment can reveal mistaken beliefs about yourself—deeply held unconscious views and perspectives—and the resultant clarity can free you from restrictive and even destructive habit patterns of thinking, feeling, and acting.

Your Gift to Others: Embodying and Enacting True Belonging

There is great pain and great need everywhere in our world. The distress of others is often palpable, and the extent of suffering in the world is beyond imagination.

In a real sense, the power of presence and the peace and understanding you discover in your journey toward true belonging are precious gifts you can begin to offer to ease the pain of others and the heartache of the world. Your gifts of presence and compassionate response need not be a painful burden or a heavy responsibility for you, nor must they drive you on some kind of impossible rescue mission. Rather, these wonderful gifts will emerge naturally and find beautiful expression through simple practices of mindfulness and compassion and the actions that you take in response to nonjudging awareness and the understanding it brings.

Finding self-awareness, peace, and understanding within also immediately illuminates your possibilities for benefiting others. The answers to such questions as "How can I help?" or "What needs to happen next?" almost always can be discerned and acted upon more effectively when awareness and compassion have been cultivated and when understanding emerges, moment by moment and situation by situation.

As the meditation teacher Sharon Salzberg notes, "Our view of who we are, what we are capable of, what matters in the world, molds our intentions, which in turn mold our actions. How we look at our lives becomes the basis for how we act and how we live and whether our choices are shaped by love and kindness" (2008, 7). Salzburg thus suggests that "how we look at our lives" is crucial for living a life linked to our deepest values and best qualities.

This book looked earlier at the power of conditions in the inner life, including deeply held views, to shape and even hijack you into distorted perceptions and actions. It also has explored the importance of using mindfulness practices to bring each of these inner life elements into awareness.

Once in awareness, your habitual patterns of reaction—which may also be perpetuating feelings of loneliness and separation—can be better managed, and new possibilities for happiness, as well as for experiencing the power of belonging and connection, can arise. And as you shift into these new possibilities—and act from them—the beneficiaries will likely be others as well as yourself.

A good example is what happened with one woman who came seeking help with managing her weight and tendency to overeat. In a meditation class, she took part in a raisin-eating exercise, in which each person receives three to four raisins and is asked to eat each raisin, one at a time, while bringing mindfulness to every aspect of eating it.

This woman held her first raisin, looked at it, smelled it, placed it in her mouth at first without chewing but just feeling it in her mouth, then biting into it, chewing, and noticing the sensations and tastes as the raisin disappeared and was swallowed. She did the same process with each of the remaining raisins.

When she returned a week later for the next class, she reported what had happened at home: "I was at home with my kids watching television one night, and I had a big bag of junk food open in my lap and was eating from it when I remembered about that raisin. So I started to eat the junk food mindfully, and guess what happened! First, I realized I didn't like the taste of the junk food! Then, I realized I was not even hungry. I was just upset.

"Well, I closed up the bag and put it away. Then I turned off the television and started playing with my kids, and we had a nice time."

Indeed, embodying awareness includes being mindful of what is happening in your body. In this case, the woman noticed she didn't like the taste of the junk food, and she was not even hungry but "just upset."

Enacting true belonging includes breaking free of the perceptual prison of separation and upset within, using awareness and intention, and consciously embracing the connections available in the moment. When the woman put away her junk food and was able to engage with her children, not only did she benefit, but her children did as well.

The Preciousness of Each Moment

The conditions and relationships in our lives are impermanent, and life is fleeting. Many people, as they face life-threatening illness or tragedies, speak of the preciousness of living and of relating more deeply to others, and they lament how it took the threat of losing their lives (or loved ones) for them to finally start paying attention to how precious it all is.

When you look closely at the impermanence and frailty of life and of your relationships, you see that you actually do have a choice. You can contract and withdraw inside, falling into the quicksand of dread, fear, or avoidance, or you can turn toward the truth of change, awakened and engaged, motivated by the deep understanding that it is life's very impermanence and frailty that makes each moment and relationship so absolutely precious.

Then, perhaps by accepting the truth of change and mortality, moment by moment, day by day, and relationship by relationship, this realization will awaken even deeper feelings in you of gratitude and awe at the mystery of being alive and will accordingly nourish in you a widening sense of responsibility for growing self-awareness.

In the understanding that we are all already deeply interconnected, you might then become motivated to practice cultivating mindfulness and qualities of compassion, kindness, and generosity not just for your own well-being but very much for the peace and well-being of others.

As the contemporary Zen master Thich Nhat Hanh has said: "When you produce peace and happiness in yourself, with the conscious breathing that you produce in yourself, you begin to work for peace in the world. To smile is not to smile only for yourself; the world will change because of your smile. When you practice sitting meditation, if you enjoy even one moment of your sitting, if you establish serenity and happiness inside yourself, you provide the world with a solid base of practice. If you do not give yourself peace, how can you share it with others?" (1988, 51–52).

Looking Ahead

So far, this book has been exploring a map of the inner life as revealed by mindfulness, with particular attention to perspectives and deeply held views about self and situations.

You have seen how those perspectives are actually only a part of the landscape of the inner world and are impermanent, yet they hold great power to shape perceptions and can distort your understanding of any experience you have. Rigidly held views and perspectives can also have a negative impact upon the intentions you form, the actions you take, and your effect on others.

You have also seen how awareness can be cultivated using mindfulness, how increased self-awareness can illuminate new connections and possibilities, and how this increased awareness can give rise to a deeper sense of responsibility for acting from your deepest and best places.

The time has come to pose a question: Does true belonging also mean taking your rightful place in the web of life, consciously, moment by moment, guided by the knowledge that you are already part of that web and that your very intentions (and their resultant actions) impact the others connected to you in the web?

How could you make sense of this question in terms that could translate and guide you in choices of daily living? Is this question about the web of life and your place in it merely philosophy, or does it point to something more?

As you engage with and explore the practices in this book, in your own way and in your own time, you will discover what true belonging means for you.

It is a journey only you can make, and it is yours to take.

part 1

connecting with yourself:
practices for deepening
awareness

1   It's Like This, in You—"Yes!"

It's easy to become caught in habitual interior reactions when something stressful happens, and most especially when an interior reaction is unpleasant (characterized by fear, worry, sadness, or pain, for example). That reaction in mind and body can become a momentary (or extended) universe marked by familiar habits of thinking and feeling, including deeply rooted inner narratives focused on yourself that are critical, alarming, and despairing.

Such reactions to stress usually occur outside of your consciousness. They are revealed only by the actions or words they stimulate and drive you to express.

Often, both the internal and the external habitual reactions to a challenge or a stress are ones of ill will and aversion. Some interior vocal part of you demands that the situation be different—whether the challenge or stress is a physical one (such as sore muscles, a headache, or fatigue), someone in your life (an irritating neighbor, a demanding customer or client, or a sick loved one), or an external event (a job loss, a natural disaster, or a political argument).

Until you can shine the light of awareness on these reactions and stop reinforcing them, you will be doomed to remain their prisoner.

The following practice—using the phrases "it's like this" and "yes"—can help you use mindfulness to cultivate a different habit—one of radical acceptance to moment-by-moment experience. By *acceptance* in mindfulness practice, we mean dropping the fight—at least for the moment—and being willing to let things be and to see them as they are.

Practicing acceptance means being willing to stay present and conscious and using mindfulness to explore your feeling of aversion instead of letting it drive your responses. For example, you might notice the sensations of ill will and aversion arising as reactions in your body, or you might notice the tone of your voice and the content of your thoughts. If you can disentangle yourself from strong feelings of aversion, something inside might let go long enough for you to be able to move ahead with a different view, plus effective action, marked by greater understanding and more compassion.

You can use this practice either as a formal meditation or in the midst of everyday life.

⌒ reflective practice: "It's Like This, Yes!"

Decide or remember to be mindful and to practice cultivating acceptance. Pause on purpose, bring closer attention to any sight, sound, or sensation, and become conscious of dropping into this moment with awareness. Remember, especially, to include and notice any conditions in your interior environment. You don't have to do anything else except notice.

Wherever your attention lands, acknowledge what you notice with a gentle whisper of "it's like this," pause and notice and breathe mindfully, and then meet whatever you notice with acceptance by inwardly adding the word "yes." For example, if you notice *my mind is racing with worry*, whisper "it's like this," take a mindful pause, breathe, and whisper "yes." Or, if you notice *having a conversation with my friend*, then whisper "it's like this," and pause, breathe, and whisper "yes." If you notice *eating my lunch*, then whisper "it's like this," pause, breathe, and whisper "yes." If you notice *I am feeling angry and alone*, whisper "it's like this," pause, breathe, and whisper "yes." Whatever you notice, mindfully acknowledge it, pause, breathe, and allow it in this way.

Practice keeping your attention focused on the situation. As you repeat the phrase "it's like this," let it help you restore and maintain your mindful focus on the experience of the present moment. Take a few mindful breaths, pausing to anchor your attention in the moment. Use the word "yes" to support you in being open to, allowing of, and less reactive to any experience that is unfolding.

Practice being patient. You can always take necessary action later. This practice of yes is about stopping and noticing, reducing reactivity, and deepening awareness by cultivating acceptance.

You might repeat what you've said: "yes, this is worry," or "yes, this is talking with my friend," or "yes, this is eating lunch," or "yes, this is feeling angry." And keep noticing.

As in all of these practices, relax and let your practice be a journey of discovery and illumination, knowing you cannot do it wrong or make a mistake!

2 "Not Me, Not Me"

Loneliness is often influenced by self-critical thoughts. You might notice that the times when you feel most disconnected and separated from others are frequently the times when you feel most down on yourself. Dark self-loathing or criticism might cloud your mind with thoughts such as *I am worthless. I am unlovable. There is no one here who cares about me.* These spiraling negative thoughts are like imaginary roadblocks that distance you from yourself and others.

If you want to break free, you must recognize that deep connection with others starts with cultivating the connection from within.

In the Hindu tradition, the Neti Neti meditation offers a unique mantra for experiencing your world and letting go of discouraging thoughts about not being good enough. Neti Neti translates literally as "not this, not this"; another commonly used variation is "neither this nor that." The following meditation is used as a way to redefine and reconceptualize what something is not.

reflective practice:
"Not Me, Not Me"

Find a comfortable place to sit and connect with your breath. Pay attention to your breathing. Are you holding your breath? Are you breathing through your mouth or your nose? By being with your breath and fully connecting with the rise and fall of each in-breath and out-breath, you are returning to the power of the present moment of all there ever is and its magical unfolding, right here and right now.

Next, pay attention to your thoughts and feelings. You may have many different kinds of thoughts, some important, some mundane, some superficial. After each thought, tell yourself, *I am neither this nor that. This is not me. This thought is not reality.* For example, you may feel desperately all alone, but in reality you are not truly alone. The world is widely inhabited, and you are surrounded by other people. From another perspective, your feelings do not dictate who you really are; they are simply emotions that rapidly change in importance at any given moment. In truth, you are much, much more than the thoughts, feelings, and upsetting reactions that cross through your mind.

In fact, your thoughts are merely versions of reality that may or may not be true. You can free yourself from the trap of unwanted or untrue thoughts.

You might want to recollect with mindful attention several self-critical thoughts that you have experienced in the past or notice with mindful attention such thoughts if they arise during the meditation, such as *I am useless. I am a failure. I am never good enough.* As each negative thought appears, tell yourself, *I am not this.* What you are saying, in effect, is *This thought is not who I am; this thought is not reality.*

Try using these words in a mantra each time a depressing feeling or thought surfaces. Your mantra script might go as follows:

> *Negative feeling:* I am depressed about how lonely I feel.
>
> *Neti Neti mantra:* I am not this. This thought is not who I am. This thought is not reality.
>
> *Negative feeling:* I hate how isolated I feel. I feel excluded from fun things.
>
> *Neti Neti mantra:* I am not this. This thought is not who I am. This thought is not reality.

Remember, the point of this practice is not to relive past disheartening thoughts but to engage in the present moment by acknowledging what you feel right now. You can make this a sitting practice for five to ten minutes once a day or simply employ the Neti Neti mantra throughout your day as you notice self-critical remarks enter your mind. Over time, as you drop the discouraging thoughts, you'll open doorways for connection with yourself and others.

3   Caring for Your Pain

Pain in this life and in these bodies is unavoidable. But the suffering you experience—related to pain—is optional.

There is a crucial distinction between pain and suffering, and it arises in how you relate to pain. As a wise meditation teacher once pointed out, suffering equals pain multiplied by resistance. In other words, the more we each resist, make war on, or deny the pain we feel, the greater is our suffering around that pain.

Claude Anshin Thomas went to Vietnam at the age of eighteen. He was a helicopter door gunner and by his own estimate killed hundreds of people and endured horrific experiences in the war. In his book, *At Hell's Gate: A Soldier's Journey from War to Peace*, Thomas describes how the seeds of his suffering related to violence began in childhood, carried on and multiplied in the war, and came home with him from Vietnam.

For years after returning home, Thomas was unable to sleep at night due to anxiety and hyperarousal based in memories of his wartime experiences. His sleeplessness became a serious problem. Thomas recalls how he tried many times to escape his pain, turning to drugs and alcohol because he couldn't accept the "whole of myself, including my anxiety." Finally, he found that practicing mindfulness helped him live "intensely" in the present moment, and eventually, he "simply accepted this fact: I can't sleep." In that moment of acceptance, Thomas "felt a peace I have rarely experienced before. A peace with my unpeacefulness" (2006, 63).

Finding "peace with my unpeacefulness" was Thomas's path to healing. Dropping his resistance to the pain ended his suffering around it.

You too can use mindfulness and compassion to explore healing any pain you are bearing. It is possible to change your relationship to pain, to learn to include it and allow it as part of your wholeness, and, by dropping your resistance, to nurture healing and peace in your life. Try the following meditation.

∿ reflective practice:
Caring for Your Pain

Set your intention to work mindfully with some pain that is burdening you, physical, mental, or emotional. Don't demand any "fix." Just be curious and willing to be surprised.

Take a position that supports your body comfortably during meditation, and choose a place where you are likely to remain undisturbed.

Breathe mindfully for a while, gathering and steadying your mind and opening your heart to this moment.

When you feel ready, deliberately bring to mind the pain you have chosen to reflect upon,

65

breathing mindfully with a broad focus that acknowledges, admits, and allows each of the feelings, thoughts, and bodily sensations that arise associated with the pain.

Pay attention steadily and closely, perhaps beginning to notice the tone of your thoughts and any feelings of ill will or anger toward the pain that may be present; remaining open and attentive, allowing those feelings as well; holding and including them in the light of your awareness.

Return to your mindful breathing as often as you need to, steadying your focus more each time and keeping your heart open as you notice and include all of your experiences—arising and changing—in this moment.

Let courage, strength, and equanimity also support you as you maintain a close, steady focus. Keep breathing and watching, mindfully noticing the changing sensations, thoughts, and emotions related to your pain in each moment. Notice any insights you have, as well.

When you notice resistance to your experience arising, practice explicitly dropping the resistance, perhaps by quietly whispering to yourself something like "I recognize the anger [or fear] I feel for this pain, and I know that this pain is with me in this moment. Breathing mindfully, I drop the fight, make room for this pain to stay as long as it needs to, and continue watching it."

Breathing mindfully, practice allowing the total experience to be just as it is, repeatedly dropping any fight against the pain as you continue watching.

You can end your meditation whenever you feel ready.

What have you learned by watching and meeting your pain with more acceptance instead of ill will? What lessons does the pain in your life have to teach you?

4   Nourishing Your Hunger for Connection

Meals are a time of deepening the ties that bind us all together. Dinnertime with family, perhaps more than any other meal, can unite us. But what if you eat your meals alone every day and night? Or what if family dinners have lost their vital spark and have turned into dinners eaten separately or in silence in front of the television? What if such meals leave you feeling discouraged and disconnected?

If you hunger for connection, simply acknowledging what you're thankful for can help you reconnect with yourself and others. The practice of giving gratitude and acknowledging your appreciation can happen at any moment. You can say a prayer of gratitude while you're chopping vegetables or standing over a hot stove with your kids screaming or music blaring in the background. You can write something that expresses your inner feelings of what you're happy for and then recite it at every meal by yourself. You can speak your gratitude aloud randomly and spontaneously each time you place an item on the table as you prepare for a meal.

reflective practice: Nourishing Your Hunger for Connection

What are you thankful for? Identify five to ten items that are right in front of you, either in the kitchen or at the dinner table. Let it be about anything your heart and imagination wish to notice. Here are some suggestions:

- "I am so happy that I can enjoy this meal with my wonderful partner."

- "I am so happy that my cat can join me for this meal today."

- "I am so happy that my kids are having fun right now and not fighting."

- "I am so happy that I didn't burn this meal and it tastes great."

- "I am so happy with my new slow cooker that made this meal."

- "I am so happy that I have a dessert to look forward to after this meal."

- "I am so happy for sharp knives, a good cutting board, and a great cooking pan."

- "I am so happy that I am able-bodied and can prepare this meal without help."

- "I am so happy when my teenager washes the dishes."

- "I am so happy to be fed, nourished, and full."

Say whatever you are thankful for, silently to yourself or aloud.

Repeat this practice as often as you can think of doing it. After only a few minutes, you may actually experience a rise in positive energy flowing from within and a growing sense of appreciation for every little thing in your life. Giving thanks unlocks your ability to feel connected and fulfilled by the simplest of things.

5   The Gift of Forgiveness

On this journey of life, you carry a mental suitcase brimming with a countless array of emotions. The ones that weigh the least—generosity, inner peace, kindness, love, happiness, and the like—carry little emotional burden. The ones that weigh the most—resentment, anger, guilt, a sense of unworthiness, hatred, and the like—burden you the greatest. These difficult emotions leave you feeling unfulfilled, incomplete, and often stuck in the past.

The heavier emotions are frequently based on long-unresolved issues and old grudges which are difficult to release. Some emotions begin with self-centeredness and thus increase the gap between self and others, which then leads to loneliness.

When all this baggage starts to weigh you down and becomes an obstacle to deepening your connection with others, it's time to lighten the load. The easiest way to shed the weight of destructive emotions is to offer forgiveness.

Forgiveness is a meaningful and lasting gift that you can offer yourself and others. The following meditation will assist you in developing your special powers of forgiveness, which will lead you to a greater sense of inner peace, courage, and harmony with all things and beings.

◌ reflective practice:
The Gift of Forgiveness

Find a place to sit and relax. To become fully aware of the present moment, simply follow your breathing. Pay attention to the coming and going of air in your lungs, the movements of your diaphragm, and the sensations in your abdomen. Do this for at least five to ten breaths.

Now, imagine yourself struggling to walk while lugging a large and bulky bag with no wheels. This heavy bag is full of your resentments. Using mindful awareness, explore a particularly troubling feeling that you have. You may feel resentful about the pressures placed upon you by an aging parent. You may feel anger at your child for ignoring your advice and getting into further trouble. You may feel disappointed by a friend who didn't include you in some detail of his life.

Take this mindful moment first to offer forgiveness to yourself: *May forgiveness fill my heart and space. If I caused any harm or pain, intentional or unintentional, I offer forgiveness to myself.* As you offer forgiveness to yourself, you are freeing yourself from clinging to the past in the hopes of drawing others closer. Imagine your bag of resentments getting lighter. You are starting to walk with more comfort, ease, and steadiness.

Next, imagine asking for and offering in return openhearted forgiveness to another person. Perhaps you had a falling out with a parent, sibling, partner, or friend. Since you have no control over another's actions, reactions, or feelings, your offering of forgiveness must always remain open and without attachment to expectations or outcome: *May this offering of forgiveness release us from our previous misunderstanding. If I caused any harm or pain, intentional or unintentional, I ask for forgiveness. I offer forgiveness and understanding in return. May compassion guide us to a better understanding and bring us closer.* As you offer forgiveness to others, notice any emotions that arise. Imagine your bag of resentments loosening off your back, freeing you to move with less resistance and negativity along your path.

The practice of forgiveness opens you to the compassion in your heart. If you practice it daily, old resentments will dissolve. The gift of forgiveness opens the heart, and an open heart melts the separation between you and others.

6   Calm Body, Quiet Mind, Steady Attention

Meditation teachers since ancient times have recognized that learning to focus and sustain attention upon a single object—a sound or the sensation of the breath, for example—is a crucial element in training the mind and heart in meditation.

As attention is trained through practice, and as it is maintained and sustained on a single focus, you become more relaxed and at ease: better able to remain present with awareness; less distracted by thoughts, feelings, sounds, or sensations; and better able to see clearly exactly what is present and unfolding, breath by breath.

Studying individuals who practiced meditation, cardiologist Herbert Benson reaffirmed the ancient wisdom of this practice. Benson (1975) documented that when attention is placed and sustained upon a neutral object or focus in meditation, your mind and body are capable of a *relaxation response*, where heart rate and breathing can slow, muscles can relax, and the mind can become quieter.

The following meditation is an invitation to explore directly the power of concentrated attention for bringing ease to mind and body—and for amplifying awareness—through formal meditation practice. You will notice that its basic steps follow those of the mindfulness-of-breathing practice found in the Foundation chapter.

We encourage you to explore this practice deeply. Use it to establish a firm connection with the present moment and to bring the depth of your inner life into penetrating awareness.

∽ reflective practice: Calm Body, Quiet Mind, Steady Attention

Choose a place to practice where you can relax and will not be interrupted.

Assume a position that supports your body comfortably and also supports alertness. If you are sitting, you might check that you are upright, not slouching or slumped forward, that both feet are on the floor, and that your head, neck, and back are all in good alignment.

Gather awareness in your body, beginning by simply noticing the changing sensations in the different regions and body parts.

When you are ready, gently bring attention to your breath sensations and practice awareness of breathing as you have learned to do it. Remember to relax, allowing your body to breathe naturally as you soften and invite the sensations of each breath to come to you.

Practice taking a narrow focus on the breath sensations, letting your attention become increasingly sensitive and precise as you notice the sensations at the beginning, the middle, and the end of the in-breath.

Practice establishing a continuity of attention by staying with the sensations at the end of the in-breath, noticing a pause, continuing attention, and noticing the beginning, the middle, and the end of the out-breath. See if you can remain present for the moment when the sensation of the very last movement of the out-breath fades into stillness, and continue your attention into the stillness, as well.

Whenever you notice your mind has wandered from the focus on the breath sensation, just notice where it went without adding anything or fighting what happened. You have not made a mistake. Gently and patiently return your attention to the sensations of your breathing.

If you like, after practicing for a while with the concentrated focus of attention on the precise and subtle sensations of breathing, you can expand your focus—making more room in awareness—to consciously accept and include sounds, other sensations, and thoughts and feelings. Keeping your attention on the breath softly and gently, patiently practice breathing with each of these other experiences, especially the unpleasant ones. By resting attention lightly on the breath as you breathe with your unfolding experience—and allowing whatever comes into your awareness to be just as it is—you may notice that you become steadier and are not fighting or following the changing experiences so much. You may also find that you notice more clearly how each of these experiences is not "you" but rather is constantly changing and impermanent, including the most intense or alluring ones.

You may continue as long as you like. Simply end your meditation by bringing attention back to your surroundings.

Notice how you are feeling afterward and how it changes as you move forward into and through your daily activities.

7   "Ah, This Grand Body of Mine!"

Physical exercise is one way to reconnect meaningfully to this beautiful and magnificent body of yours. Another way is this next practice, which will help you reconnect with your body by noticing the little miracles it performs every day. You can do this practice anywhere and anytime you're in motion: working out at the gym, walking to your car, washing dishes, or folding the laundry.

∾ reflective practice: "Ah, This Grand Body of Mine!"

The next time you're in motion, focus on your breath. Each breath is an opportunity to reconnect with the ever-present moment of now. Each breath is powering your body's ability to follow through on your next desired movement.

Imagine each breath giving life to the body you use every day for so many tasks and demands.

Now, be mindful of your body in motion, however subtle—the bend of your wrist, the feel of your foot making contact with the ground— and acknowledge it. For example, the next time you lift your arm to reach for something, acknowledge what your body does for you by thanking your body: *Thank you, arm. Thank you, wrist. Thank you, hand.*

In this step, follow another movement of your body, however subtle or small. For example, pay close attention to the next blink of your eye. Imagine the number of muscles and nerves that are coordinating within your body to execute this important activity—the movement of the lid, the sweeping motion of the lashes, the moistening of the cornea, and so on. Take this moment to acknowledge your body: *Thank you, brain. Thank you, eye. Thank you, vision.*

Take this small moment to celebrate your body that has served you so faithfully and enduringly. Think about how it has been a dedicated ally and aid to you all of your life: *Thank you, body! Thank you for your endless service.* There is only you and your body here now, in this moment. *Ah, this magnificent body!*

Make it a daily practice to acknowledge the many miracles that your body performs—breathing, dancing, running, singing. Recognize and appreciate the work your body does for you, every little movement, from head to toe.

When you make time to marvel at the extraordinary gifts of your body, you deepen your connection with yourself.

8   A Value-Driven Life

This is your life. For the most part, it consists of what you value. For example, if you value friendship, then you might prioritize being someone whom your friends can turn to in times of need; you will take time to listen, be present, and show you care. Your values shape how you see the world and how you see yourself in the world. Here is a guided visualization to help you pay attention to what you value and how your particular values can improve your sense of connection to yourself.

∽ reflective practice: A Value-Driven Life

Bring your awareness to your breathing and the constant flow of air passing in and out of your nose, mouth, lungs, and entire body. In each breath, you are strengthening your relationship to this instant in time. You may notice an array of thoughts and feelings arise. Resist the impulse to label them as good or bad. If you find yourself reliving the past, return to the breath and focus on the natural rhythms of each in-breath and each out-breath. Next, bring your attention to your values.

Ask yourself: *What do I value most of all?* Make a mental or written list. Start with your relationship with yourself. What might your values reflect if you focused on you? You might answer: *I value myself. I value my body. I value my health. I value my intelligence. I value my self-sufficiency.* Take a moment to sit and meditate on the values that come to mind. These values give meaning and significance to your life every day. Continue to be mindful of your breathing.

Now, expand your relationship circle to include others. Try to imagine your values reflecting a life that is less alone and more connected.

What might your values be if you centered them on connectivity and interdependence? You might answer: *I value love. I value people. I value peace. I value respect. I value honesty.* A value-driven life is a life that has purpose, and it's a life in which you actively participate in cultivating the values that reflect the life that you desire. Imagine your values mirroring the best parts of yourself.

Once you have taken the time to consider your core values, the next step is putting them into action. For example, if you value love, tell someone today that you love her. Act on your value by sending an email, letter, or text, or by phoning. If you value connection, then consider what you might do to bring others into your life in deeper and more meaningful ways, such as an invitation for lunch.

Remember, when you're feeling lonely or disconnected, to check in with what your values are. Then notice if you're embodying those values by acting on them.

Taking the time to notice if you're living your values can reconnect you with what you care most about. Acting on that information can make you feel more connected to yourself and the world around you.

9   Path to Joy

Abraham Lincoln said, "I have noticed that folks are generally as happy as they make up their minds to be."

If only it were that easy, you say. If only you could think yourself out of these dreaded feelings of loneliness and isolation when they creep up.

What if we told you that happiness isn't a special place or a perfect partner or a situation that lasts for several years? What if happiness were right in front of you, in this single moment, and only one breath away? The following meditation will help you cultivate inner happiness—maybe not the ecstatic joy of a winning lottery ticket or of your son or daughter getting married—but a quiet and calming inner pleasure that resides in you and is there whenever you need it.

You can do this practice at work, in your car, or sitting quietly and resting at home, or whenever you want to take a happiness break.

ᖾ reflective practice: Path to Joy

> Bring your attention to your breath. In this one breath is life. In the next breath is life renewed. In the next breath is life replenished. Each breath returns to life over and over again.

Now take a moment to think back on a happy memory, a time when you were truly joyful, when the feelings of elation and laughter bubbled inside your very being. That happy memory might be finding out that you were accepted into college or that you were going to have a baby, or it might be the day you met your best friend. As you breathe and recollect that special moment, pay attention to how the memory makes you feel. You might feel a little giddy, sentimental, hopeful, or reflective. You might experience a sensation of smiling inwardly or a warm glow of joy and contentment. Let those feelings wash over you.

Visualize walking up to a mirror and smiling into the face of those heartwarming sensations circulating within you. See yourself reflecting the lightness and happiness in that single moment in front of the mirror. Take a few more relaxing breaths before you go about your day.

This exercise is not about getting stuck in your past or reliving old memories. You are taking a mindful pause for positive, patient, kind reflection. Whenever you find yourself feeling down, remember to breathe, return to a joyful memory, and smile. Joy resides in you—ready for you to tap into it at any point.

10   Opening into Awareness

This formal meditation practice is another invitation to explore and connect deeply with the fullness of this moment and your life unfolding, here and now, with mindfulness. This practice is especially useful for learning to connect more steadily and closely with the changing experience of your mind and body.

Take as long as you like. Consider giving yourself the opportunity to relax and really settle in, in a time and a place where you won't be disturbed for a while.

∽ reflective practice:
Opening into Awareness

Take a comfortable position, one that can sustain you for the time of your meditation.

Relax, and put down any thoughts about changing or becoming anyone else or any thoughts about "doing meditation."

Realize that meditation is not about doing anything at all. It is about being, and about knowing something about what is happening now and here. Ideas of fixing, striving, or becoming carry you off into an imagined future, away from now.

Recognize that—in this meditation—you have taken a seat in the middle of your life, as it is unfolding right now; you are paying attention and coming to this practice with a sense of caring for yourself and a dignity that honors your status as a living, breathing, unique human being.

Perhaps sit with a spirit of investigation and welcoming attention, with an attitude of trust in yourself and confidence in your ability to notice with clarity and increasing sensitivity what is arising for you in this moment, without judging.

Now, bring attention to the sensations flowing through the different parts and regions of your body. Allow yourself to feel the sensations just as they are—a pressure, a vibration, a contraction or an expansion; warmth or coolness; moisture or dryness; the touch of a breeze or the texture of your clothing against your skin.

When you notice your mind filling with thoughts or wandering, you have not made a mistake. You don't have to fight your thoughts or blank your mind—and, you don't have to follow or feed your thoughts, either. Simply notice the thoughts, letting them be, letting them go, and returning attention to the sensations flowing through your body.

If you like, you can narrow your focus onto the sensations of this breath flowing into and out of your body. Find the place where you feel this breath sensation most easily, allowing yourself to feel each sensation and bringing your attention back, very patiently, to this breath sensation whenever it wanders or is drawn away.

Let each breath sensation come to you, relaxing into awareness in a way that allows the meditation to support you.

Continue to rest in awareness, letting your body breathe naturally and knowing and allowing the changing sensations of each breath. Notice and allow also the changing sensations in your body, the changing sounds, emotions, and thoughts passing through this moment.

Calmly abiding, steady in the knowing awareness itself, observe and allow the changing conditions until your meditation period ends.

By holding the total experience of your mind and body in mindful awareness, gently, patiently, and breath by breath, you can realize the truth of being more consciously in your body and alive, and you can enjoy a moving experience of true belonging.

part 2

connecting with others:
practices for understanding
and caring

11   Remembering the Animals

A man speaks in reverent tones of sitting on his porch, late at night in darkness, and watching animals passing on his lawn. "It's like a spiritual experience," he says.

In a supermarket, a child picks up a package of hamburger meat and asks her mother, "Where does hamburger come from?"

Individuals on a retreat gather to bless their food before eating. Two lines from a Buddhist blessing emerge: "Countless others gave their lives and energy that we may eat. May we be nourished that we may nourish life."

Living in this world, we all have many complex interactions, connections, and relationships with all living things, and especially animals. Some people minimize these relationships, regarding animals as inferior or only as sources of food, entertainment, or transportation, yet spiritual teachings in many cultures regard animals as guides and teachers.

Saint Francis of Assisi considered animals to be brothers and sisters in God's creation, and he addressed them accordingly.

Anyone who has lived with and cared for animals on a daily basis knows they have awareness, are alive in the moment and in deep touch with their senses, and can express a range of emotions.

Dogs, cats, and other animals can make a powerful therapeutic impact on the lives of lonely and isolated people in nursing homes, prisons, and hospitals, as well as on the lives of those who live alone but have pets or animals as companions.

The following meditation is an invitation for you to reflect mindfully on the presence of animals in your life, your views toward them, and your relationships with them.

∽ reflective practice: Remembering the Animals

Choose a place where you will not be disturbed or interrupted, and take a comfortable position.

Breathe mindfully for a few moments, letting your mind and body become calm and opening into a space of clarity and kindhearted awareness.

Now, bring to mind a relationship that you have or have had with an animal. Let yourself imagine and sense the animal, how it looks, sounds, and smells, and how you interact.

Continue to breathe mindfully as you reflect on this animal and your relationship, noticing memories, thoughts, emotions, and anything else that comes into awareness as you reflect.

Stay with the focus, resting and looking more deeply with each mindful breath.

When you feel ready, release the image of this animal, continue breathing mindfully, and shift attention to a different animal.

Feel free to investigate. This second animal could be an animal that you do or don't know, one that you do or don't like, one that is happy or in distress—or even one that is threatening. Breathing mindfully as you reflect on this second image, let yourself notice all that you associate with this image.

Conclude your practice by reflecting on the insights you have gained.

Let the insights from this practice support and guide all of your relationships. Those insights might include:

- the power of memories in your mind and body

- the distortions caused by fear

- the freedom to choose that follows awareness

12   A Fingerprint of Love

Physical or emotional pain can hinder your ability to feel connected. Since such pain is internal, others may fail to see or comprehend the challenges that you face, leaving you feeling alienated and disconnected.

When you feel this way, what single act would allow you to feel more connected to others? You might answer "a hug." But what can you do to reconnect with others when a hug is not readily available?

What if every loving embrace, however brief, actually clung to you in some way? What if the sense of contact lingered on in your heart long after the physical embrace ended?

The following meditation will help you appreciate the flow of warmth held in every cuddle or squeeze and deepen your sense of loving connection with others long after the hug has ended.

↷ reflective practice:
A Fingerprint of Love

Find a quiet place to sit and relax. Close your eyes and follow the steady rhythm of your breathing. Notice the cool air passing in and warm air passing out.

Take a moment to recall a good hug that you experienced with someone you care about. Maybe it was with your child or with your friend or with your grandmother. Imagine the embrace as if it were happening right now. Pay close attention to every part of that hug. Notice the pressure of the squeeze between the two of you. Notice the way that person feels against your body. Notice his or her scent. Is it spicy? Sweet? Notice the way his or her skin feels. Is it soft? Warm? Notice how you feel in this embrace and what sort of emotions come up for you. Do you feel comforted, safe, loved?

Now, take a moment to explore what intentions are exchanged in every hug. Perhaps you hug people to convey your support or tenderness, or you do it just because you are happy to see someone. Imagine those intentions still clinging to your clothes, to your body, to your skin for a long time after the separation.

Take this mindful moment to offer your gratitude: *I am grateful for every embrace. Each embrace has left its lasting imprint of love and affection. I am thankful for every touch of kindness in my life.*

What if every embrace didn't wash off or dissolve, as you might have thought? You may feel lonesome, but that last hug is still with you, absorbed into your whole being. Each hug is infused with love and remains with you.

With each embrace, you leave a lasting imprint of kindness and tenderness with someone, to be offered and passed along to the next person.

13   The Source of All Life

Life cannot exist without water—not you, not the trees, not the animals, not the coral reef. Babies are made up of 78 percent water, and adults consist of nearly 60 percent water. Water has even been detected in the Milky Way. Water connects every living thing.

You know all this, you say, but you still feel lonely. The following mindful meditation will help you recognize your connection to this source of all life and deepen your relationship to all forms of life.

reflective practice: The Source of All Life

Find a comfortable place to sit, relax, and close your eyes. Take several deep, full breaths and then return to your normal breathing pattern.

Take a moment to notice what's going on around you. There may be a number of distracting sounds, smells, or movements in your vicinity. Let that be okay. You don't need to fight the disturbance or commotion. Just notice what it is. Perhaps a plane engine is roaring overhead. Perhaps you can hear the clamor of wrestling children in an adjacent room. Perhaps you can smell a pot of coffee being brewed near your office. Let it simply be.

Now, take a brief journey to better understand the source of your connection to everyone and everything through a basic element of life. For example, suppose you have a glass of water in front of you. Where did this water come from? Follow it back to its hypothetical source. Your water comes from your faucet, likely getting there through pipes traveling from your water municipality, which gets its water from a nearby fresh water source, such as a river, reservoir, or well.

Imagine the water at its source. Imagine the fish that swam in it, the elk that drank from it, the rocks that were shaped by it.

Before you take your next sip of tea or water, remember that each of us is drinking from the same water that replenishes all life. Drink with grateful satisfaction that each drop of water links you to all life, and offer a blessing: I am one with all life in our shared need for water and replenishment. With each sip, may this water connect me to the world in deepening and profound ways.

When you trace the essential elements of life— water, soil, air, sunlight—you begin to see how closely linked you really are with all living things. You share in the sources of life with so many others.

14   Fall in Love with Life

Falling in love is an intoxicating and passionate experience. Have you ever been in love? Do you remember the sensations of your heart aflutter at the mere mention of your lover's name or the sound of your lover's voice? Do you recall how the day felt brighter and more hopeful, the air fresher and sweeter, and your life more memorable and alive?

Being in love seems to exhilarate and enliven your everyday routine. Being in love opens the heart, which allows you to be more available and loving toward others.

What if falling in love weren't reserved for just someone you know or someone you necessarily have romantic feelings for? Could you imagine falling in love with a field of wildflowers or an ancient redwood forest or a river that flows to the sea? The following meditation will inspire you to fall in love with life, which will help you to channel all that passion and awareness into loving others. It is important only that you tap into this loving energy. Let it guide you and emanate from within you, and then share this love with others.

reflective practice: Fall in Love with Life

In this ever-present unraveling moment, there is just this one breath, and the next one. Focus on each breath now. Simply follow the breath without changing or altering it. Each breath is a single moment in the now.

Next, bring to mind a time when you were feeling, giving, or receiving love. It may be a romantic time spent with your partner. It may be the last hug you gave to a friend. It may be a love letter you received a long time ago. Recall the feelings of love that washed over you. Those emotions are still circling and swelling in your heart.

Now imagine offering that love in silent spirit to someone around you. Pick anyone. If there is no one around, find a tree or a cat or a flower that catches your eye. Select anything and bestow your love upon it. From the center of your heart, allow yourself to fall in love with this person, place, or thing.

Speak your intentions aloud or to yourself: "May this love encircle one and all." Imagine the free fall of love, the expansion of your heart, the wide-open potential for hope and desire. You are tapping into the universe of love that unites all beings in the world. Now give it away. It is your gift. It asks for nothing in return.

You can fall in love every day, with your life, with others, with the cosmos. Love is the essential truth behind the how and why of human connectedness.

15 Belonging to the Natural World

The beauty of nature and the natural world is almost always a good place to start when you need a stabilizing focus for steadying your attention and for reflecting on themes of belonging and interconnectedness. How you connect with that natural beauty, especially through mindful attention, can be illuminating and transforming.

Who has not paused to marvel at a beautiful sunset or to wonder at the night sky or to smile at a bird calling its companions? Our attention seems naturally drawn to such natural beauty, and feeling touched by it, the mind relaxes a bit, and the heart can soften and open.

In such moments, it may seem like your usual ego boundaries disappear, and you can feel yourself expanding into and being part of something much larger and more beautiful—present here and now—something that you were not aware of even a moment ago.

The great conservationist and world traveler John Muir had such experiences. To him, the natural world was a source of wonder—marvelously diverse and alive—and a place of refuge, relationship, and belonging. In his memoir, *My First Summer in the Sierra*, Muir writes of his experiences guiding a herd of sheep in the Sierra Nevada in the summer of 1869. He points to a sense of the interrelatedness of living things.

"When we try to pick out anything by itself we find it hitched to everything else in the universe" (1997, 157).

Muir felt a deep sense of connection with all forms of life in the wilderness, and his interaction with life there was a very personal one. When his human companion, Mr. Delaney, had to leave him, Muir wrote: "Felt not a trace of loneliness while he was gone. On the contrary, I never enjoyed grander company. The whole wilderness seems to be alive and familiar, full of humanity. The very stones seem talkative, sympathetic, brotherly" (238).

The good news is that you don't have to travel to Yosemite or go back in time to feel your connection with nature and other living things. The wonder and beauty of the natural world are here for you, now.

◌ reflective practice: Belonging to the Natural World

Set an intention for yourself to pay closer attention and to become more mindful of the beauty of the natural world around you, and practice often with that intention for a period of time— an entire day, perhaps, or a week, or longer, if you wish.

You might begin simply by deciding to stop more often, notice, and connect with natural beauty when you encounter it. For example, instead of walking past a tree, a plant, or a flower, you might stop, take a few mindful breaths, and pay closer attention to it—for even a few breaths. What do you see?

Or upon seeing a bird, an animal, or a sea creature, or upon noticing busy insects, recall your intention to connect more deeply, and pause—breathing mindfully and disentangling from your train of thought long enough to look more deeply into the life expressing itself directly in front of you in this moment. What is happening?

Or take time to stop and gaze at the clouds or the stars in the sky, really looking at them with new curiosity and interest. Breathing mindfully, notice and release the chatter in your mind and the gripping and tension in your body, and relax into the awareness that simply notices with clarity and sensitivity. What do you become aware of?

If you like, keep a journal of your mindful observations of nature, recording any insights or joys that reconnecting with natural beauty and life brings to you.

Let mindfulness be your doorway to reconnecting with natural wonders—and your own natural goodness and beauty—every day of your life.

16   A World of Smiles

Supposedly it takes fewer muscles to smile than to frown. But smiling isn't always easy, because a smile involves more than mere muscles.

A smile is a nonverbal form of communication that reveals emotion, human happiness, even vulnerability. But a smile can also be a gift, an offering to others that can switch someone else's horribly stressful day into a sweet moment, in the blink of an eye.

A smile from a passerby can be infectious. You may have noticed that when you smile, people frequently open doors for you and appear to listen more intently when you're talking. As the adage goes, "Smile, and the world smiles with you."

The next meditation is for nurturing your ability to smile. You can practice this when you're alone or with a friend or in public with strangers. You might come to discover unexpected and mysterious ways to connect with others—offering your silent understanding, as well as acknowledging and affirming them—just by offering a smile.

reflective practice:
A World of Smiles

Bring your attention to this mindful moment by reconnecting with your breath, inhaling through your nose, and exhaling through your mouth.

Now, bring a smile to your face. No smile is too big or too small, too crooked or too perfect, too sexy or too misleading. Just give yourself permission to smile and to imagine a warm glow of kindness radiating outward. You don't need a reason to smile. Simply smile because you can!

Bring your awareness to the sensations in your face and observe what feelings come up. How does it feel to smile intentionally? Do you feel silly, awkward, self-conscious, or a little giddy? How do others respond to your smile? Without judging yourself or labeling it as good or bad, continue to smile for longer and longer periods.

If someone is in pain or feeling down, your smile may offer kindness and caring. Set your intention with every smile: *With this smile, I am offering compassion to others. With this smile, I am offering my understanding without imposing on someone's space or privacy. May this smile connect the two of us in deeper ways.*

After you have smiled for at least three to five minutes, take some time to notice how you feel. Are you feeling more peaceful, more serene, more open? When you smile, do you feel you have your guard up, or do you feel your defenses beginning to dissolve?

Practicing smiling, whether on your own or around others, is a powerful tool for changing how you feel. Imagine your smile as a pool of happiness and understanding that you can dive into throughout your day—it's always there for you, just waiting for you to dive in and share.

17   "We-ness"

When you are in the throes of loneliness, there is a desperate and isolating feeling of only "I." You may find there is little room in your dark cave for a "we." In fact, you may have gotten very good at keeping everyone else out. If you stay there long enough, you may entirely forget that there are others who are feeling the same as you—alone, scared, cut off, detached. How do you shift your perspective and discover the "we" in your loneliness? It can help to remember that at the core of our humanity, we are more alike in our emotional struggles than we at times care to admit.

The following meditation is for developing a sense of "we-ness" when you feel locked in a prison cell of loneliness. This practice is best done in public.

◌ reflective practice: "We-ness"

Find a place to sit comfortably. Begin by being mindful of your breathing; observe each breath as it flows in and out of your lungs and body.

Now take in your surroundings—the sights, smells, sounds, and sensations. Notice the people, the grass, the shadows or the reflections on surfaces. Notice the aroma of nearby food or beverages or plants. Notice the hum of voices around you or the distant sounds of traffic. Notice the wind or the warmth of sunlight.

What feelings arise for you? If feelings of loneliness surface, observe them with tenderness, patience, and compassion.

While you hold tender space for your loneliness, take a look around you and notice other people who are nearby. Imagine at times that these people feel alone, afraid, and disconnected. Imagine that they too want to feel a sense of belonging and oneness, as much as you do. There is a "we." You and those people that surround you are included in this "we." We are in it together. We belong to the same humanity; we share the same emotions and desire to connect. We have much more in common than we often acknowledge.

Take this moment to offer a blessing to others: *May you know that we are not alone. May you know that we are linked in powerful, emotional ways. May you feel the "we" in this silent moment with me. May we feel it together.*

When you acknowledge your feelings are connected to others' feelings, you are actively engaged in creating unity, community, and a sense of "we-ness." There is only a "we."

18 "Stop and Stay with Me"

You can tell when someone is not really present with you in a conversation or activity, can't you? Something seems missing, and the feeling of connection and presence isn't there. And, these days, an ongoing conversation might be interrupted at any moment by a phone call, a text message, or some other intrusion that disrupts the sense of connection.

These examples serve to remind us—perhaps because we keenly notice it and miss it so in our own relationships—that presence is one of the greatest gifts we can offer another person. Presence is about maintaining attention that is still, steady, and alert. It is based upon having the intention to actually be present, and it deepens with a commitment to maintain your connection despite interruptions.

Presence also depends on connecting with a spirit of generosity in your own heart, because being truly present requires mobilizing your willingness, kindness, and courage to include and allow another's experience to be just as it is, and not be driven to change or fix anything simply because you are feeling momentarily distracted, bored, or upset by what the other person may be communicating.

Being present also depends on stopping, moment by moment, and setting down your own habits of outer and inner busyness. It calls for focusing and sustaining attention in a way that includes all of what is happening: the other person, your inner life, and the unfolding experience arising from your interactions, moment by moment.

The following practice will help you cultivate a deeper presence in relationships, with others and for yourself.

∾ reflective practice: "Stop and Stay with Me"

Set an intention to practice being more present in your relationships. It could help to approach this practice with curiosity, without judging yourself, perhaps asking, *What would it be like to pay more attention and to be more present, for another person and for myself, moment by moment—even a little more often than usual?* You can practice anytime you are with someone else, in any form of communication, or just when sharing time together, by taking the following steps:

1. Remind yourself to stop and stay in the present moment. Breathe mindfully, and return to the present moment with patience for yourself when your attention wanders, remembering to include yourself, as well as the other person, mindfully in your field of attention.

2. Bring attention back repeatedly and connect with the sensations of your breathing. Let

your mindful breathing be an anchor that stabilizes you in the present. Letting yourself notice your breath sensations from time to time during the conversation, by taking a mindful breath as you listen or before you speak, can open a new dimension of presence and awareness, from which you can observe and connect with the other person and grow in self-awareness, as well.

3. Keep your attentional focus light and broad as you continue breathing mindfully, remembering to include your own body sensations and posture, as well as any pleasant or unpleasant feelings you may be having, in your noticing. It can help to recall that you don't have to "fix" anything that you are noticing, but just remain curious, keep watching, and let things reveal themselves.

4. Practice listening mindfully to the other person's words as he speaks, and listening to your own inner reactions as well.

5. When your turn to speak comes, listen to yourself more closely, as well. When you have finished speaking, resume your practice of mindful breathing, and remember to notice your inner world as you listen and remain present for the other person.

6. Whenever you feel disconnected, have curiosity about how and why that happens, without making it a problem or someone's fault. Just notice, especially your own thought train and emotions, and let them go. Come back to a mindful breath.

7. Let your intention include attempting to restore the connection when you notice it is broken. Mindfully notice what happens as you reengage with the other person and how you reengage, practicing patience and compassion as you do.

Remember to allow your practice to be soft, kind, and curious. Remember that presence is a gift, not an obligation.

You can do this practice for as briefly as a single mindful breath or throughout an entire conversation or an entire relationship! There is no right or wrong way. Let curiosity and intention motivate you, and let mindfulness inform you, as you explore deepening presence in all your relationships.

19   Containers for Connection

When you are lonely, everything around you can appear life-
less, estranged, and detached from its original joyful association. It can help to focus on certain objects to reconnect to
joyful moments past, particularly things you associate with
others. Some of the memories that lie within can be important reminders of those who care about you. The following
meditation is best done in a place that is familiar to you, such
as your bedroom, living room, or backyard—a place where
the objects around you are easily identified.

∽ reflective practice:
Containers for Connection

Begin with bringing your awareness to your
breath. Notice the expansion of your belly on the
in-breath and the emptying of your lungs on the
out-breath. Follow your breathing for five to at
least ten full breaths.

If you are in a familiar room in your home,
take this time to visibly scan the area. If you are
not in a familiar place, close your eyes, select
a room that you know well, and begin to look
around. Make a mental list of what you notice in

the room, such as a bed, chair, bookcase, cabinet. Go deeper and take note of the little things, such as potted plants, sculpture, paintings, a quilt, or photos. They may be small everyday items.

Among these various objects, focus your attention on one that holds a particular meaning or importance for you. Perhaps a movie stub on your desk reminds you of a recent fun outing with your family. Perhaps a photo of your son or daughter at a graduation reminds you of how deeply proud you are of him or her. Perhaps a postcard on your refrigerator is from a close friend who was thinking of you and sends love.

Take this time to be mindful of what your association is with the object. You might want to make a written or mental list of those associations. For example, movie stub = good times and laughter; photo = reminder of celebration of accomplishments; or postcard = reminder of love and friendship.

With your list of objects and associations in mind, set your intentions: *May these objects serve as reminders that I care about others. May these objects serve to remind me that I am surrounded by others' care and compassion.*

Each object contains a memory that holds the power to remind you of how each passing moment can be filled with connection to others. In fact, the connections you miss most of all may be closer than you think.

20   Dissolve the Boundary

You can't see the walls—they are not made of thick slabs of concrete or secure steel bars—but you feel them intuitively. Everyone, at certain times, erects walls of defense to keep others out or to keep them from getting too close.

There are, of course, times when such walls are necessary and appropriate for protection, but sometimes these walls take hold elsewhere in your life, closing you off from others unintentionally. If those boundaries stay rigid and secured for too long, you might convey the wrong message, such as *I am not approachable. I am better off by myself.* Sometimes the boundaries that you have constructed to protect yourself become the walls that keep you from opening up to others.

Here's a meditation for dissolving the walls that continue to separate you from new people and experiences. You can do this meditation at home, outdoors, waiting for the bus, or standing at a busy intersection.

∽ reflective practice: Dissolve the Boundary

Start by connecting with the breath. As you inhale, feel the cool air sweep into your lungs. As you exhale, feel the warm air brush past your nose. Focus on your breath for five to at least ten full breaths.

Wherever you are, consider what your invisible walls might look like. Make a visual sketch of your walls. For example, your walls might look like a white picket fence, like plain chicken wire, or like plastic bubble wrap. These imaginary walls walk with you wherever you go—the market, the bank, the shopping mall, the park, and social gatherings.

Now visualize yourself in a safe place, physically dismantling your barriers. Imagine your fence evaporating into thin air or your concrete barricade crumbling to the ground. You put up your walls, and you can decide to take them away when appropriate. Behind them is just you and your open heart.

When you dissolve these barriers, you offer a new message in their place: *I'm openhearted. I am open to giving and receiving. I am connected to others.*

End this meditation with a few cleansing breaths. Notice if you feel more of an openhearted connection to the world around you.

You can choose which boundaries you want to keep and which ones aren't necessary. When you dissolve your barriers, you are promoting a message to others that you are open and available and that you care. Other people will pick up on these subtle cues and may surprise you with their openness and availability.

21   There Is Always Silence

In our busy modern lives, the notion that silence could be at the center of our being may seem somehow ridiculous or at least inaccessible. Yet, awash in the relentless noise, have you ever longed for silence or wished with all your heart for some peace and stillness within?

If so, pause for a mindful breath and consider a different perspective on noise and silence. What if silence is always here and you just fail to notice it—perhaps in some way similar to how you don't see the forest for the trees?

Perhaps all it would take to hear silence would be to pay attention and to disentangle yourself from the insistent stream of noise and chatter in your mind and heart. You may enjoy exploring silence in your own life with the following meditation.

reflective practice: There Is Always Silence

Take a comfortable position and breathe mindfully for a few minutes. When you feel ready, shift your attention from the breath sensations to the sounds around you.

Listen mindfully to hear the near sounds and the far ones, opening equally to all the sounds.

Relaxing, with attention focused on the different sounds as they come to you and depart, allow the sounds to wash over and through you, noticing as they arise and fade away.

Gently observe any thoughts that arise about the sounds, without fighting or following the thoughts; simply notice them and let them go, coming back very patiently, as often as necessary, to refocus your attention on the changing sounds.

As your attention to the sounds becomes more precise and steady, allow yourself to also notice the silence before and around each sound.

Let yourself become increasingly aware of the silence as well as the sounds.

As you listen more closely, perhaps begin to notice how each sound arises from the silence and returns to it, like a wave arises from the ocean and returns to it, never truly separate or disconnected, but always interconnected.

As you become increasingly familiar with the presence of silence amidst all sounds, see if you can find it more and more often, turning to and resting in silence as a support and a refuge in any situation. Learning to rest in silence opens the possibility of less distraction, more sustained presence, and appreciation of caring and connection—in you and with others.

part 3

taking mindful and
compassionate action in
the world

22   Practicing Peace

How often does some preexisting view, belief, or memory tilt your entire being toward dehumanizing (and disconnecting from) another person? When this happens—in conversation or in the middle of an activity with others—what thoughts, words, or actions result? How are feelings of separation and isolation reinforced? What toxic perceptions are sustained?

Or, if you carry biases from your own background—and we all do—how quickly does a frustration or challenge, for example, on the job or in a chance street encounter, associated with your biases evoke a dehumanizing comment?

How can you locate the part of yourself that dehumanizes others, understand and heal the trauma it represents, and engage each person you meet with *pro-social*, instead of anti-social, behaviors? How can you disentangle yourself from interior habits of war-making, of isolating and criticizing based in unconscious or misinformed fears and prejudice, and learn instead to acknowledge others without ill will, perhaps joining them in relationships that allow and work with differences—relationships that neither enable future victimization nor feed stereotypes or perpetuate hatred?

Such change in perception and action can take enormous courage, compassionate self-awareness and acceptance, and a sharp capacity for clear seeing.

Roshi Bernie Glassman is a widely respected Zen teacher and the founder of the Zen Peacemaker Order, an organization devoted to exploring and teaching ways to make peace, one moment at a time. Glassman has led many retreats to Auschwitz for individuals from war-torn cultures. He uses the place and the horror and intensity of what happened there in his effort to promote healing and peacemaking, and to broaden and deepen retreat participants' understanding of an enormous reservoir of wisdom and compassion available within each of us.

In *Bearing Witness: A Zen Master's Lessons in Making Peace,* Glassman writes about the retreats: "As our relationship with Auschwitz changed, so did the relationships among ourselves....And people spoke....Some told of abusive fathers, former soldiers who wouldn't talk about the war, who drank to forget" (1998, 32).

When the American-born son of a Jewish concentration camp inmate met the German daughter of the Nazi commandant of that same camp, eventually they talked and "discovered they had many things in common, including shame, guilt, and silence. The expected anger of that first meeting had eventually evolved into a deep and powerful bond of understanding and empathy, and finally into a strong, meaningful friendship" (28).

You can explore releasing ill will and practicing peace more intentionally in your own life, using the following meditation.

∽ reflective practice:
   Practicing Peace

Set an intention to explore and make peace with your own biases and fears concerning particular people or situations. Do this in a spirit filled with generosity, curiosity, and compassion, not with any quality of self-judgment or recrimination.

Begin your practice of peacemaking whenever you notice feelings of anger or fear arising within you related to a certain person or situation. It could be a person or situation in your life or one you have heard about.

As soon as you become aware that you are reacting with anger (or fear), recall your intention to practice peacemaking, restrain yourself from impulsive words or actions, and begin breathing mindfully.

As you feel your attention settling more on your breath sensations, notice any thoughts or emotions you are having. Remember that you don't have to fight your thoughts and you don't have to follow them, either. Rather, allow yourself simply to listen to the angry or frightened thoughts and narratives unfolding in your mind as you continue breathing mindfully, and let them be.

It could help to name the experience you are feeling, breath by breath, such as *This is anger.*

This anger is in me now. These thoughts and feelings are how anger lives in me. Continue mindful breathing as you notice and name the feeling. Can you see it changing? Can you feel it changing in your body, your heart, your mind? Make the experience of anger a focus of interest and curiosity rather than a problem or an identity, and keep watching it.

Continue to breathe mindfully, asking, *What keeps anger alive in me?*

Listen for any interior responses that may arise. Repeat this question a few times if that helps, listening each time for more thoughts and feelings as you continue mindfully breathing and remaining present and aware of all that is happening.

When you have learned something about what feeds the feeling in you, try some other questions. Recall the person you started with: *Could they have feelings or thoughts like mine? What keeps anger alive in them? Are we so different?*

Finish by breathing mindfully as you reflect on one last question: *How can I change?*

Engage this practice whenever you wish, without judgment or attachment to any specific outcome, choosing instead to be curious, mindful, and compassionate, moment by moment.

125

23   Sending Goodwill

Your life experience can affect your ability to trust and connect with others or to feel compassion for them. In a world of uncertainty and violence, it is common sense to be careful and cautious. But what if the distrust is so ingrained in you that you never reach out? This distrust may have developed into a kind of social anxiety, leaving you feeling lost and friendless. You may strongly desire to connect with other people, neighbors, and coworkers, but you feel paralyzed by fear. Thankfully, there are silent yet powerful ways to help heal the wounds of isolation and disconnection that separate you from others. The following meditation is a mindful and compassionate gesture of goodwill.

⌒ reflective practice:
Sending Goodwill

Begin by sitting quietly and bringing your attention to your breathing. Notice the air coming in and the air going out. In and out. In and out. Now, allow your inhalation to lengthen and draw in more and more slowly. Then exhale slowly. Try doing this for five to at least ten full breaths.

Next, bring to mind someone you are having difficulty connecting with, perhaps a friend, family member, coworker, or neighbor. When you have a clear image in mind, return to your breath. In your next out-breath, visualize your breath carrying the feelings and intention of goodwill to that person.

Offer the following blessing: *May you be surrounded by generosity and goodwill. May your life be filled with benevolence and harmony.*

The next time someone comes to mind whom you want to connect with, send this person goodwill as you exhale. You can practice sending goodwill every time you face a situation that produces distrust or discomfort.

When you send a blessing of goodwill, you spread caring and hope to others. Practiced daily, goodwill draws you closer into the web of all life and opens the doors for trust and connection to deepen and expand.

24   Listening Anew

Listening to others is the key to deepening your loving connections. Unfortunately, over time, listening skills can become impaired until you're no longer actually listening to what another person is saying. You may hear only what you want to hear. You may half listen to your parent's advice and then quickly disregard it. Maybe you've lost friends or ended a relationship because of problematic communication, unresolved arguments, or long-held disagreements.

Listening is a skill that can be developed. It can lead you to great clarity and to building intimacy with others. Listening requires that you be present. When you are fully present, you become more aware and focused, which allows you to be a better listener.

The following meditation will help you brush up on your ability to genuinely listen and respond with mindfulness and compassion. It does not ask you to relive the past but to recollect with caring attention a time when communication with someone was troublesome.

reflective practice:
Listening Anew

Begin by noticing the gentle rise and fall of your breath. The rise and fall of each breath helps to ground you in the present moment.

Take this moment to recollect a time when you were having a difficult conversation with someone. You may have had an unresolved issue with your partner. You may have had a misunderstanding with a friend. You may have had a disagreement with your boss.

Try to imagine coming together with a willingness to listen anew. As you recall the conversation, allow yourself to engage in the same dialogue as if you've never heard it before. You are listening with new ears, new insights, and an openness to possibilities for resolution and understanding.

You may tell yourself the following: *I am listening with an open ear and an open heart. I am listening to you with a fresh mind—without judgment and with a clear perspective.*

Picture your new dialogue flowing with ease and respect. Picture kindness flowing out of your heart toward the other person. Imagine that both of you are listening to one another with the awareness that each sees the world in unique ways, for no one is right and no one is wrong. Visualize the conversation ending with a sense of understanding and acceptance of each other.

Every time you listen well, you move toward someone and you build companionship. Every opportunity to listen anew is an opportunity to feel less frightened and lonely. When you truly listen with openness, you see the world differently. Astonishing things happen when you can listen from the heart and observe others with conscious and compassionate attention.

25   "How Can I Help?"

It's a familiar story—the White Knight comes to the rescue. Into the midst of a crisis, for example, when a loved one is dying, or a family emergency erupts, the relative or friend who has not been all that involved suddenly appears, assumes command, and pushes for things to be done his or her way. What is going on?

Studies in palliative care and end-of-life care have discovered that caregivers often suffer from *empathic hyperarousal*, a chronic stress reaction. It comes from being exposed to the suffering of another when little can be done to relieve it, so your empathy for another is repeatedly and intensely evoked with little promise of relief. The distress of constant stress and empathetic hyperarousal, if poorly managed, can drive people into reactive and unwise (even hurtful) words and actions. Although the White Knight may have been neither physically present nor involved, he may have nevertheless been suffering from intense distress, simply from the knowledge that a person he cares about is sick and dying, and this distress may drive behaviors that are off-putting to others.

In addition to empathetic hyperarousal and chronic stress, psychologists and family therapists have found that adults are often still working out their relationships with other family members, and periods of extreme stress, like the death or illness of a loved one, serve to amplify these unfinished interior struggles. In this case, the White Knight may be carrying some of these struggles as well, bearing some old family conflict that now, in a period of distress, drives him to show up and try to fix things.

Whatever the deeper motives, in practically every White Knight case, someone is hijacked into very self-centered and self-serving behaviors—in the name of "helping"—because intense and uncomfortable interior feelings and personal stories are dominating his moment-by-moment reality of thoughts, emotions, and actions.

Compare this self-centered suffering-dominated approach in the context of helping others with an approach based in self-awareness, self-care, and an intention to help that comes from generosity and is actually focused on the needs of others.

You might call this second approach *selfless compassion*, because it is not driven unconsciously by a self in distress, but rather is motivated and energized by the deep human qualities of kindness and the desire to relieve the suffering of another.

The paradox of this selfless compassion is that it depends upon nurturing and sustaining a wise and compassionate relationship with yourself. For example, becoming free of empathic hyperarousal requires the courage and skill to bring your ego-self and the personal narratives and feelings related to it into penetrating awareness, recognize these narratives and feelings when they are demanding attention, and disentangle from their urgency. Selfless compassion also depends on your ability to befriend any feelings of upset and pain you may feel and to develop effective skills to soothe those feelings as they arise, especially in difficult situations.

So, learning how to first take care of yourself—through awareness and self-compassion—might be the best way to be an effective helper and caregiver to those who really need your help. The following meditation can help you help yourself and others.

reflective practice: "How Can I Help?"

When you find yourself in a situation where someone needs help, explicitly set an intention to be as helpful as possible.

Begin breathing mindfully and connect more consciously with your inner experience— thoughts, emotions, and bodily sensations, especially—as well as the context you are in.

If it helps, quietly name or note to yourself what you are noticing, such as *I am here in the hospital room. I am breathing mindfully. I notice fear and worry in me. I notice the upset on the faces of those around me. I hear the sounds. I smell the smells. I continue breathing mindfully. I keep noticing.*

133

Relax and continue mindful breathing and silently naming all that you are noticing, as this moment and this situation that you are a part of continues to unfold around and within you. Relax and allow yourself simply to notice whatever you can, settling more steadily into this moment with mindfulness, compassion, and kindness.

Be especially alert for any judgments, self-centered views, or angry commands that arise in your own mind and heart, and practice naming them, letting them go, and not reacting to them.

During the times that you are waiting and not being very active or engaged, come back to mindful breathing, relax, steady yourself, and simply watch with compassion as your inner and outer worlds unfold, breath by breath.

Protected by mindfulness and compassion, moment by moment, maintain your connection to the changing situation. When you are ready, try quietly asking yourself, *How can I help?* Then listen mindfully for all of the responses before taking any action. Let wisdom and compassion guide what you do.

Remember to do this reflective practice during difficult times when you want to help but don't know how. The person you help might even be the White Knight!

26   For Those in Need

Natural disasters happen seemingly with greater frequency with each passing year. You may be aware of the growing number of tsunamis, hurricanes, floods, and famines that have occurred in distant places around the globe—from New Orleans to Indonesia to Haiti. These are terrible tragedies that affect innocent lives. Each person lost is precious and cannot be replaced. You are affected emotionally even if you are not there.

You may know a friend or coworker who is worried about his or her family who survived a natural disaster. You may have fond memories of a vacation you once spent in a place that was hit by a terrible fire.

When disaster hits, you may feel powerless and helpless. You may feel angry at nature and wonder how this could happen and how can it be stopped. Here is a meditation that will help you make peace with the strange and mysterious forces of nature and respond compassionately to other humans and nonhumans who are suffering.

∽ reflective practice:
For Those in Need

Seated comfortably and with your eyes closed, check in with your breathing. On the in-breath, say aloud or to yourself "in." On the out-breath, say aloud or to yourself "out." Do this for five to ten breaths.

Now, bring to mind a recent natural disaster. Without judgment, mentally note what feelings and sensations come to the surface. Perhaps you feel tearful, stressed, worried, mournful. Perhaps you feel confused, furious, impatient, hopeless. You may experience a tightening in the neck or back or a feeling of heaviness in your body. Do your best to recognize and name the emotion or sensation without calling it good or bad. Simply be present with the various thoughts and reactions that you are having.

Now, say the following aloud or to yourself: "May these feelings of concern and compassion within me touch the people and places of those most in need." You may want to repeat these words as a mantra several times with slow and deliberate intention. Take a mindful moment to remember that nature doesn't have a preconceived plan to strike with force, and thus you have no control over the mystifying ways that nature works.

Take another mindful moment to remind yourself that your life is entwined with all beings and all of nature around the world. You are not alone in your feelings of sadness but are joined by a global outpouring of love, compassion, and resources. We are all united on this spectacular planet, spiraling together through space. Visualize your love, tenderness, and concern nourishing others and bringing them comfort. Your kindness and caring are assisting those who need it the most.

Given the complexity of natural disaster and the emotions that may surface for you, this meditation will take time and repeated practice. What is important in your practice is to remember that you are not alone with your worries, concerns, or fears. People from every country and continent are pooling their resources through prayer, contributions, and resources to help others in need. When you set your intentions to send compassion and healing, others will feel it and join you.

27   Global Network for Love

Today you can call a friend in China, email a business colleague in London, and text message your son in Chicago. People and places that once seemed out of reach are merely a fingertip away. But that doesn't mean that you never feel lonely. You may have 352 friends on Facebook, but do you really feel more interconnected in the ways that foster emotional closeness and intimacy?

Your day may contain many activities, such as driving, shopping, cooking, and cleaning, that you do alone. A sea of people in your apartment building, neighborhood, job site, and supermarket might surround you, and yet you may struggle with feeling alienated and isolated emotionally. Fortunately, there are ways to feel more interwoven into the global fabric of life. The following loving-kindness meditation will help reconnect you.

∾ reflective practice:
Global Network for Love

Find a place to sit quietly and comfortably to begin. In this moment, pay attention to your posture. Notice where your back rests against the seat. Notice any muscles that are tightened or strained. Take this time to relax and settle into a comfortable position. Next, be aware of your breath. Take a few minutes to listen and experience each breath. Focus on your chest and your heart with growing awareness.

Imagine breathing directly from the center of your heart, as if all experiences and feelings were generated from this place. Do this for five to at least ten full breaths. Then, staying in the flow of these heart-filled breaths, repeat to yourself the following blessings of loving-kindness. If you like, say them several times:

May all beings in the world be safe and protected. May all beings be free from danger and out of harm's way.

May all beings in the world be happy. May all beings be free from mental suffering and stress. May all beings experience joy in their heart and laughter in their bellies.

May all beings in the world be healthy. May all beings be free from physical trauma or pain. May all beings feel strong and vibrant.

May all beings in the world live in peace and contentment. May all beings be free from war and violence. May all beings live joyfully in coexistence. May it be so.

Allow yourself to feel a river of tenderness, concern, love, and genuine warmth for yourself and others. End your meditation whenever you are ready.

A loving-kindness mantra will support you in the realization that all people, around the world, want and deserve the same things. All people everywhere want to be happy, safe, healthy, and in peace.

28   Your Beautiful Place

Modern neuroscience has discovered that the human brain changes with how you use it. Circuits used more often grow stronger while those that are not engaged actually wither as brain connections weaken. This capacity of the human brain to change with use is known as *neuroplasticity.*

Indeed, practicing kindness can shape your brain and alter your perceptions, moment by moment, in positive ways.

See for yourself how adding an explicit practice of friendliness—by intentionally wishing yourself and others well—might affect your life and relationships as they continue to unfold. Such practices of loving-kindness can be especially valuable resources when stormy emotions cloud your mind and heart and sweep you away into feelings of isolation and separation.

reflective practice: Your Beautiful Place

Let this practice serve you both as a formal meditation practice and as a brief informal reflective practice in daily life. As a formal practice, it could be done as follows.

1. Establish yourself comfortably in a location where you will likely not be disturbed. Take care to turn off cell phones, pagers, and other devices, and let those around you know that you wish not to be disturbed for a while.

2. Take a comfortable position, and explicitly set your intention to explore the practice of loving-kindness.

3. Begin by practicing mindful breathing for a while. Putting down any busyness or desire to change anything about yourself, releasing any judgments or impatience that may be lingering, simply rest attention on your breath sensations and gather your awareness here in the present moment.

4. After a time, shift your focus and imagine that you are in a beautiful place in nature. Let the image of that place saturate your heart and mind. It is your favorite place, possibly a beautiful beach, or a tranquil lake, or a majestic mountain.

5. As you imagine yourself located in this beautiful, favorite place, let it fill all of your senses. What do you see (colors, shapes, motion)? What do you feel (coolness, warmth, breezes, moisture)? What do you hear? What do you smell? Relax and take

your time. Let your imagination complete the image of your favorite beautiful spot in nature.

6. As you settle more and more completely into your beautiful place, notice how happy and at ease you are beginning to feel. Let that joy and ease fill you. Bathe and luxuriate in that feeling of ease and well-being, of beauty and joy.

7. Now, bring a loved one or a group of loved ones to mind. Invite them to join you in your beautiful place. Watch how their faces light up with joy as they join you. Let their joy feed your joy. See how they relax and enjoy the beauty and richness of this beautiful place. Notice their smiles. Hear their laughter.

8. Invite others to join you. They could be anyone you like, and as many as you like, because this beautiful place is so big it can hold them all. In fact, it is so vast that it could easily hold the entire world.

9. Continue resting in and enjoying your beautiful place, sharing the beauty, the ease, and the joy with everyone you have invited in.

10. In the midst of your joy and well-being, allow yourself to realize that this beautiful place—your beautiful place, this vast place of joy and beauty—is in your own heart!

11. Continue practicing loving-kindness, resting in and offering joy and beauty for as long as you like, ending your meditation by wishing yourself and all your dear ones great happiness and well-being.

This practice is one of several in this book aimed at helping you to cultivate the mental qualities of kindness and generosity. Let any one of these practices that appeals to you become your friend and ally on the path of true belonging.

29   The World in a Bite

Imagine seeing your connection to others in a bowl of rice.

If you go through your day on autopilot, the daily routine of eating often becomes mundane and uninspiring. Whether it's breakfast on the go, lunch at work, or a microwave dinner in front of the television, you may forget to appreciate the food on your plate.

Yet every meal is an opportunity for cultivating a spiritual relationship with the food you eat. The following meditation brings mindful attention to the wondrous gifts of foods that Mother Nature provides, keeping you alive and giving your body strength and energy, one bite at a time.

reflective practice: The World in a Bite

Before you gobble up your next bite, put your utensil down and take a few mindful breaths.

With your plate of food in front of you, just sit and observe. Take notice of the colors, aromas, textures, temperature, and details. Now, choose one thing out of your meal—yogurt, lettuce, meat, apple, cheese—and study it carefully. Pick something that captures your attention and ask,

Where did it come from? How was it grown? Who grew it? Who packaged it? How did it get to my grocery store? Imagine the seed resting in the soil that was kissed by the sun and doused by the water, which gave this food its life. Imagine the birds and insects and flowers that also helped in the germination and growth of the plant that feeds you.

Take this moment to contemplate where your food came from before it reached your plate. It could be a cow grazing on the prairie or a field of corn or a fruit tree in your backyard. It may have come from California or Florida, Mexico, or New Zealand. It may have been trucked in or brought by train or plane. You may have purchased it from a supermarket or a farmer's market, or it may be leftovers from last night's dinner out. Nature plays a role in the miracle of this meal. Many people orchestrated the making of it. Be a witness to the wonderment of how much energy and dedication goes into your meal.

Now, take your first bite. Savor it wholeheartedly. Experience it fully and with your undivided attention and awareness. In a single bite, you can begin to perceive the hard work of generations of family farmers who may be connected to your meal. You are eating with the sun and the rain and the farmer and the bumblebee. They are all joining you for this meal.

With practice, you will start to see how the world is reflected in every bite you take. With each bite, you become more mindful, and with each meal, your heart opens to deeper levels of appreciation.

30 Mindfully Present, No Matter What

Falling can be frightening, and it is something we humans tend to oppose. Consider this person's perspective in the following poem by April Hutchinson:

John

Even with all the tumbling
and tumbling
and tumbling
in Karate class
he never did learn to fall.

Learning to fall can be something your ego naturally resists, but it might be useful! Instead of falling, of course, the ego wants to stand up and push ahead or even strike back.

The sense of falling—and the reactive urge to resist—that the ego feels in relationships can arise from simply hearing another point of view that the I-me-mine part of you doesn't understand or agree with.

Yet, especially when you are with others, mindful awareness of your own urges to assert self-centered views can immediately empower you to open a space and to be present with more generosity for the other person. Practicing mindfulness in such moments, you can relax your heart and mind in new ways that are truly supportive, deeply life-affirming, and much more comforting than barking at the other person with your own ego demands.

For example, one of the authors of this book—Jeff—once visited a dear relative who was dying of cancer. Jeff's relative knew about his meditation and other spiritual practices, but when the topic of what happens after death came up, the relative stated very clearly that he didn't want to talk about that or about "spirit" or "religion."

Of course, this was upsetting. What Jeff's ego wanted—to offer comfort—was being rejected. Jeff found himself in an ego space of falling, and he was unsure of how to land or how to proceed.

Then Jeff remembered that his intention was simply and only to offer his presence in any way that might comfort and assist his dear one. He remembered to practice mindfulness of his own inner life and of the unfolding relationship. This allowed him to remain present and allowed his relative to be who he was in a time when that is all he was asking for.

ᘓ reflective practice:
Mindfully Present, No Matter What

Whenever you notice your ego falling (or rising) around others:

1. Breathe mindfully for a few breaths.

2. Set an intention about helping others, something like the following: *May I learn to recognize my own reactions more clearly, accept myself, and move on so that I might help others more lovingly.*

Mindfully breathing, breath by breath, you will be better able to observe any negative or upset thoughts or emotions arising in you with openness and clarity.

Remember to practice mindful breathing to promote your self-awareness and clarify your intention to help. Doing this will help you return your focus from your own reactions to the person in front of you and help you respond with more care and compassion.

31   Helping Hands

Who brought you here to this exact place in time? Surely you didn't get here by yourself. You can put on your mindfulness hat and take a journey through time to rediscover the marvelous helpers and healers who brought you into being here today. When you take the time to acknowledge these helping hands, you deepen your appreciation for them. This meditation will remind you that many have cared for you and you too have cared for many.

∽ reflective practice: Helping Hands

Pay attention to your breathing and try to be with each unfolding breath as it happens.

You may notice that the phone is ringing, the television is playing in the background, or a wind has kicked up wildly outside your door. Let it just be. You don't have do anything or change anything. Just be here right now. Simply observe without judgment or feeling pressure to get involved.

Your journey is taking you back in time, back into an egg, back inside a womb, and back into the body of your mother. That is, of course, where

151

it all began. And then you were born. Delivered into the hands of a midwife, doctor, parent, or family member. You were brought up in the world by many helping hands—teachers, counselors, relatives, friends, pets, babysitters, and so many others. This is your voyage, so take a mindful moment to contemplate each and every person or thing that has played a part in your place on planet Earth.

Think about the names and faces and identities of those who offered their assistance in bringing you exactly to where you are right now. You may include your grandparents, parents, friends, mentors, or benefactors. You may include the country you were born in or the friend who loaned you the money to start your own business and believed in you when no one else did. Who brought you here?

After you have a mental list of the people and places that have brought you here, take this mindful moment to offer them gratitude. Set your intentions with a blessing: *Thank you, one and all, for the ways that you have nurtured, cared for, protected, and assisted me to be where I am today. Thank you, one and all, for your guidance and love along this life journey.*

Hopefully, you were born of love and were nurtured with care and kindness. This practice reminds you that you didn't get to where you are alone. A multitude of hands came together to help you arrive at this moment in time. How miraculously intertwined you are with everyone and everything else!

32   River of Abundance

There is an ongoing tension in our lives between scarcity and abundance. Will I have enough to pay all the bills or have anything left over? Can I afford to take the time off from work for a little vacation? Is there enough time in my day for a yoga class or a stroll in the park? And yet there is a middle ground called sufficiency, which can offer a surprising truth in your everyday life. When you think in terms of sufficiency, you are free and capable of cultivating an attitude that in any given experience, there is enough and you are enough. You have a choice in many situations in your life to let go of the mindset of scarcity. While you may not have total control over the flow of money or time or energy, you can learn to tap into the endless flow of love within you and others.

There are, of course, times in your life when you do not feel the ever-present flow of love—perhaps after a distressing divorce or the death of a spouse or a breakup with a loved one. And yet love is within reach. This exercise is intended to help you recognize that while there are times in your life when you may dwell on scarcity and feelings of not enough, there are also areas that are ever-flowing as constant sources of sufficiency. It is a subtle shift in perspective that can illuminate you to the sources of abundance, moments of adequacy, and experiences when you've had enough, you felt complete, you felt full. Love is just one of many sources. You can bring attention to this river of abundant love with the following meditation.

⤳ Reflective Practice: River of Abundance

Begin with awareness of your breath, the gradual and constant flow of air flowing in and out of your lungs.

Bring mindful attention to the love that already resides in your heart, the love you give away each day to your friends, parents, and children. Remember that when you wish someone love in prayer, in a hug, in an e-mail, in a kind gesture toward a stranger, or in a charitable way to someone in need, you are awakening to the abundance of love in everyone and for everyone.

The first step is to consider a few of the people whom you would like to offer this love to. You may wish to send it to a parent, a close friend, or a coworker who is in hard times. You may want to offer it to a charitable foundation or your spiritual community or the American troops abroad. Once you have someone or something in mind, offer the following blessing: *May this love that resides within me always be sufficient and replenishing. There is enough love for me. There is enough love for you. There is enough love for all of us. There is always enough.*

Imagine your river of love flowing steadily and constantly. It is a never-ending source of love from which all can take and feel replenished.

The mindset for sufficiency reminds you that if you look around you and within yourself, you will find the love you need. When you remember that you are being swept up in the silent love surrounding everyone at all times, you can more easily give it away.

References

Benson, H. 1975. *The Relaxation Response*. New York: William Morrow.

Blai, B. 1989. Health consequences of loneliness: A review of the literature. *Journal of American College Health* 37 (4): 162–167.

Didonna, F., ed. 2009. *Clinical Handbook of Mindfulness*. New York: Springer.

Glassman, B. 1998. *Bearing Witness: A Zen Master's Lessons in Making Peace*. New York: Bell Tower.

Hafen, B. Q., and K. J. Frandsen. 1987. *People Need People: The Importance of Relationships to Health and Wellness*. Evergreen, CO: Cordillera Press.

Hafen, B. Q., K. J. Karren, K. J. Frandsen, and N. L. Smith. 1996. *Mind/Body Health: The Effects of Attitudes, Emotions, and Relationships*. Boston: Allyn and Bacon.

Kabat-Zinn, J. 1990. *Full Catastrophe Living*. New York: Delacorte Press.

Kabat-Zinn, J. 2005. *Coming to Our Senses: Healing Ourselves and the World through Mindfulness*. New York: Hyperion.

Linehan, M. M. 1993. *Cognitive-Behavioral Treatment of Borderline Personality Disorder*. New York: Guilford Press.

Mitchell, S., ed. 1991. *The Enlightened Mind: An Anthology of Sacred Prose*. New York: Harper.

Muir, J. 1997. *My First Summer in the Sierra*. New York: Penguin Books.

Sagan, L. A. 1987. *The Health of Nations*. New York: Basic Books.

Salzberg, S. 2008. *The Kindness Handbook: A Practical Companion*. Boulder: Sounds True.

Segal, Z. V., J. M. G. Williams, and J. D. Teasdale. 2002. *Mindfulness-Based Cognitive Therapy for Depression: A New Approach to Preventing Relapse*. New York: Guilford Press.

Shapiro, S. L., and L. E. Carlson. 2009. *The Art and Science of Mindfulness: Integrating Mindfulness into Psychology and the Helping Professions*. Washington, DC: American Psychological Association.

Thich Nhat Hanh. 1988. *The Heart of Understanding*. Berkeley: Parallax.

Thomas, C. A. 2006. *At Hell's Gate: A Soldier's Journey from War to Peace*. Boston: Shambhala.

Williams, M. G., J. D. Teasdale, Z. V. Segal, and J. Kabat-Zinn. 2007. *The Mindful Way through Depression: Freeing Yourself from Chronic Unhappiness*. New York: Guilford Press.

Jeffrey Brantley, MD, is a consulting associate in the Duke Department of Psychiatry and the founder and director of the mindfulness-based stress reduction program at Duke Integrative Medicine in Durham, NC. He has also done multiple radio, television and print media interviews regarding the MBSR program at Duke. He is author of *Calming Your Anxious Mind* and coauthor of *Daily Meditations for Calming Your Anxious Mind* and the *Five Good Minutes®* series.

Wendy Millstine, NC, is a freelance writer and certified holistic nutrition consultant who specializes in diet and stress reduction. With Jeffrey Brantley, she is coauthor of the *Five Good Minutes®* series and *Daily Meditations for Calming Your Anxious Mind*. She lives in Sonoma County.